The Worldliness of Worship

JAMES F. WHITE
Perkins School of Theology
Southern Methodist University
Dallas, Texas

New York
OXFORD UNIVERSITY PRESS
1967

Library of Congress Catalogue Card Number: 67–15136

All biblical quotations, unless otherwise indicated, are from the Revised Standard Version, copyright 1946, 1952, 1957 by the Division of Christian Education of the National Council of Churches.

Quotations from "September 1, 1939" and "Musée des Beaux Arts," copyright 1940 by W. H. Auden, are reprinted from *The Collected Poetry of W. H. Auden* by permission of Random House, Inc.

The quotation from "Crazy Jane Talks with the Bishop" is reprinted from *The Collected Poems of W. B. Yeats* by permission of the Macmillan Co., Mr. M. B. Yeats, and Macmillan & Co. Ltd.

Printed in the United States of America

TO MARILYN

PREFACE

Prefaces have degenerated. Gone is the time when they saluted the "gentle reader," wishing him well on his journey through the following pages. Today prefaces are more apt to be defenses by which the author shields himself from "the slings and arrows" of outraged reviewers. By making his apologies in advance. the author hopes to induce the reviewer to temper justice with mercy. And so no longer do prefaces appear solicitous of the learned lector's welfare, but rather they are lengthy disclaimers calculated to disarm the reviewer.

I offer no apologies for the material that follows. My only hope is that it will be of use to the reader, gentle or otherwise, who reads these pages. Most of my readers will be Christian laymen, at least this book is written with them in mind. I doubt that the book will do the clergy much harm, and indeed I will not be at all disappointed if many of them do read it. But I write primarily to help Christian laymen realize their part in one vital portion of the great reformation sweeping through Christianity. Few areas are as vital in Christian renewal as worship. Yet there are few areas in which the gap is more apparent between the ideas of Christian leaders and the actual comprehension of the same concepts by most of the laity. My purpose is to help bridge the chasm of misunderstanding, to keep the army in touch with its advance scouts.

This is not a book of answers. It is a book of questions. My purpose is to persuade my readers to reflect upon some of the central concerns in Christian worship. This is done, not too subtly, by presenting the central thesis indicated by the title. I believe a topical book may raise more searching questions than one that tries to wave its hand at every single aspect of worship. This book will succeed if it forces the reader to fight his way through to his own answers about the meaning of worship. But if he agrees with every page and goes on nodding his head in affirmation, he may soon be nodding it in sleep. Please, dear reader, don't find this book too agreeable or it will have failed its purpose!

I rejoice that the time has come when it is possible to write a book on worship with both Protestant and Catholic readers equally in mind. The only exception to this is the final chapter. I had considered entitling it: "For Protestants Only." But then I realized that in the present situation this would be the surest way to induce Catholics to read that chapter. Would that Protestants were as willing and eager to learn from Catholics about worship as Catholics have been from Protestants! I address myself to all parts of Christ's Church though I am certainly influenced, perhaps even more than I realize, by my station as a minister and seminary professor of the Methodist Church.

It may surprise some that I have made almost no reference to church architecture, though obviously this has been an important concern for those interested in worship. It would be easy to say that I do not have a great deal to add to what I have said on that subject in previous books (*The Cambridge Movement* and *Protestant Worship and Church Architecture*). But that would be an incomplete explanation. The absence of a discussion of church architecture is more nearly the result of a growing revulsion against the squandering of so much money on monumental edifices that have so little relation to the Church's mission today. There are too many things we must discuss before we talk architecture. This book is an effort to raise some of the questions that must precede, if not prevent, building.

It only remains here to thank those who have made this book possible. I am thankful that I live and work in a Christian community, the Perkins School of Theology, where so many have given so liberally of their time and learning to improve my understanding of worship. I want to mention by name Dean Joseph D. Quillian, Jr., and professors Joseph L. Allen, John W. Deschner, William R. Farmer, Victor P. Furnish, L. Howard Grimes, H. Grady Hardin, Ronald E. Sleeth, and especially Schubert M. Ogden. The help of librarians Decherd H. Turner and Mrs. John H. Warnick has been essential, as has the skill of my secretary Mrs. John Norris in deciphering my handwriting. Only an author knows how much he depends upon the patience, encouragement, and laborious assistance of his wife. My wife, Marilyn, has certainly excelled in these as well as in all other wifely qualities.

Dallas, Texas
January 1967

J. F. W.

CONTENTS

THE WORLDLINESS OF WORSHIP

I

WHY WORSHIP?

It is very easy to avoid asking basic questions about our habitual actions. Any activity which we do frequently is liable to be performed without conscious decision. This is perhaps just as well; we would hardly take the time to rehearse daily our reasons for going to work, for taking care of the children, or for resting. And yet the very frequency of such actions makes it important that we take time occasionally to examine the bases of what otherwise become routines.

One of the most common acts of the Christian Church is worship. For vast numbers of Christians worship is a weekly or even a daily action. In common with various other activities of the Church, worship is likely to become a habitual practice to which little critical reflection is given.

Our present purpose is to reflect a bit about a question so basic it rarely gets asked: "Why worship?" We will explore one area of the unexamined life to which we are constantly prone. It is entirely possible that those who do not worship have as much to tell us here as those accustomed to do so. To have good reasons for refraining from worship may indicate that the question has been considered more seriously by non-worshipers than by those for whom worship is a routine practice. Unfortunately, worship is usually either practiced or avoided without much reflection. All too often, both the worshiper and the non-worshiper act from unexamined habit.

Why worship? The question is fundamentally one of motivation. It can be rephrased: What are the motivations that underlie our activity of worship? Many of us have been attending public worship all our lives, perhaps without ever thinking through why we do so. We can best begin by describing and criticizing some common motivations for worship. Usually more than one motivation underlies anything we do, but we become aware of this only by sorting motivations out one by one.

I

One of the most common reasons people worship is because they consider it their duty to do so. They worship because they understand it to be a means of doing what is right, fulfilling an obligation or obeying a command. One may decide he worships because of a claim on him by God, the Church, a religious society, or even the civil state. To worship because one understands it as his duty is certainly to fulfill a reasonable and widely accepted motivation.

It is strange, however, that the Bible neglects to make any general commandment to do worship, though at times specific acts of worship (keeping the Passover, baptizing, etc.) are represented as based upon divine commands. Idolatrous forms of worship are consistently denounced in Scripture but blanket injunctions to worship are absent.

Even the keeping of the Sabbath began as a day of rest, a humane practice rather than a cultic one.

If general commands to do worship are lacking in the Bible, both Roman Catholics and Protestants have more than supplied this lack during the centuries since the New Testament was completed. From the early third century to the present, documents from Rome specify the times at which Christians should worship. The Protestant Reformers began a long series of similar statements within the churches of the Reformation.

Even before persecution had ended in the early Church, the Synod of Elvira (about A.D. 305) had threatened with excommunication those who failed to attend church for three consecutive Sundays. The modern obligations of all Roman Catholics to worship are summed up succinctly in the *Code of Canon Law* (1917). "On feast days of obligation," the *Code* says, "Mass must be heard; and one must abstain from servile work" (Canon 1248).[1] In America Catholic laymen and clergy are under obligations to attend mass on all Sundays and six special days. Some commentators even go so far as to define how late one may come (the epistle) and how early he may leave (after communion) and be regarded as having fulfilled his obligation.

For the clergy and those in religious orders there is the additional obligation of saying the daily office. Indeed, the very term "office" derives from a word meaning duty or service. The saying of the daily office (as from the breviary) becomes the lifelong duty of anyone ordained or taking final vows in a religious order. The *Code of Canon Law* states: "Clerics who are in major orders . . . are bound

[1] T. L. Bouscaren, S.J., C. Ellis, S.J., and F. N. Korth, S.J., *Canon Law: A Text and Commentary* (Milwaukee: Bruce, 1966), p. 700.

to recite the canonical hours daily in their entirety according to the proper approved liturgical books" (Canon 135).[2]

Protestantism has made duty a strong motivation for worship though its emphasis here has been less consistent than that of Roman Catholicism. Luther was cautious about prescribing too rigidly the forms of worship for the true Christian, though he was quite willing to affirm that God had commanded baptism and the Lord's Supper. Calvin believed God had commanded men to pray and that to refuse to do so was tantamount to denying God's promises and blaspheming.[3] The *Westminster Confession of Faith*, 1647, a basic document for Presbyterian churches, had no compunctions about considering worship and its specific forms as reflections of the divine will "prescribed in the Holy Scripture." Like other Reformed confessions, the *Westminster Confession* interpreted the commandment regarding the Sabbath (Exodus 20:8) as enjoining weekly public worship.

Anglicanism retained the ancient reference in the mass to "our bounden duty that we should at all times, and in all places, give thanks." If anyone missed the point, various civil laws saw to it that he would be in church on the Lord's Day. The *Canons* of 1604 enacted that Anglicans "keep the Lord's Day . . . according to God's holy will and pleasure, and the orders of the Church of England prescribed in that behalf" (Canon 13). In the eighteenth century John Wesley preached on "The Duty of Constant Communion" and his Methodists decreed that he "hath no more place among us" who fails to attend "upon all the ordinances of God" including "the public worship

[2]Ibid. p. 116.

[3]*Institutes of the Christian Religion*, III, xx, 13.

of God, the ministry of the Word, . . . the Supper of the Lord, family and private prayer, searching the Scriptures, [and] fasting or abstinence."[4]

In some quarters today there is a renewed emphasis on the duty to worship manifested by covenant groups that assume a disciplined life.[5] Members of such groups frequently undertake a covenant that obligates them to various observances including public and private worship. Similar groups are sometimes found among collegiate ministries in inner city parishes. The motivation to worship primarily from a sense of duty has undergone many forms over the centuries but remains very real for many Christians today.

But some questions need to be raised about this motivation for worship. Both the attitude of modern man to such motivation and the judgment of theology call for our examination.

The Church ought to respect the hard-won maturity of modern man. Is it not one of the marks of man in "a world that has come of age" that he has gained his independence from arbitrary authorities? Modern man often refuses to be convinced by a plea that something is right; he insists on knowing why it is right. To be sure, the autonomy of modern man is not an unmixed blessing, but it is a major achievement of the present age and one for which we should be thankful. The rebellion of modern man against arbitrary obligations ought to be a cause of rejoicing to the Church. Western Christian culture has played a major role in bringing man to this maturity.

[4] *Doctrines and Discipline of the Methodist Church 1964* (Nashville: Methodist Publishing House, 1964), pp. 46–7.

[5] Cf. Robert Raines, *Reshaping the Christian Life* (New York: Harper & Row, 1964), pp. 131ff.

For the Church to advocate worship primarily on the ground that it is one's duty is simply to forget that duty has very little meaning to many people today. This is most graphically shown in the reaction of young unmarried adults who are noticeably absent from worshiping congregations. They rebel against going to worship simply as a duty but are apt to return to worship when different motivations are found.

On theological grounds the sanction of "ought" must also be questioned, since it can too easily slip into a form of dry legalism. The greatness of our freedom in Christ Jesus is that one acts out of a motivation of love rather than from legal obligation. Luther sensed this in his fear of making the actual prescription of worship too firm. One does not worship because it is commanded but from spontaneous love that takes the form of corporate worship for its expression. Luther agreed with St. Paul that obedience to the law alone is insufficient motivation.

Certainly many people will continue to make duty the primary motivation for worshiping. But by itself the sanction of duty hardly seems sufficient any longer. We have reached the point of diminishing returns for advocating worship solely on this basis, and it is probably just as well. There are other and more significant, if less commonly expressed, motivations for worshiping than that of duty alone.

II

There are various reasons for worshiping that seem to have little in common at first glance. Many of them can be summed up by observing that they justify worship on the grounds of fulfilling some purpose. These motivations have in common the fact that they advocate worship as accomplishing some good end. Now doing something because it is right and doing something because it is good are not completely distinct motivations. There is a difference; the right is accomplished by obedience, the good is sought as a goal toward which one works. So we can classify some of the reasons for worship as directed to accomplishing some purpose, just as we have seen motivations directed to fulfilling one's duty.

The variety of ends or purposes sought is bewilderingly complex. We shall try to disentangle some of the more prominent purposes sought in worship, though they seldom exist in isolation. Human decisions are rarely prompted by a single motivation. The study of Christian ethics and the study of worship frequently provide parallel lines of investigation, since both disciplines are concerned with the nature and pattern of actions customary throughout the history of the Church. The study of ethics makes it very apparent how diffuse the motivations influencing an ethical choice may be, and the decision to worship may have as many ingredients.

It is possible to distinguish several ends indicated in the Bible for the doing of worship. Worship as a way of presenting one's supplications before the Lord is a frequent theme in the psalms. Sacrifice becomes a means to expiation or communion. Quite another end seems to be suggested in I Corinthians 14:26. St. Paul has been dealing with the problems of speaking in tongues and the difficulty of many in comprehending what is said. St. Paul's resolution, perhaps the oldest canon for Christian worship, is: "Let all things be done for edification." The word translated "edification" implies a building up of the Church as an end sought in worship.

One could trace various acts of worship throughout the Bible and analyze the purpose of each. Baptism brings, among other things, the forgiveness of sins (Acts 22:16). The Lord's Supper is performed for the recalling of Jesus (I Corinthians 11:24). Separate acts seem to have appropriate ends: confession, praise, supplication, intercession, and others.

Throughout the history of the Church, various acts have been directed to particular ends. The seven sacraments of Roman Catholicism share in the same grace but have particular ends for which different forms, matters, and ministers apply. Certainly a constant theme of Christian worship has been the desire to glorify God. The *Gloria in excelsis* is in a sense an epitome of all Christian worship: "We praise thee, we bless thee, we worship thee, we glorify thee, we give thanks to thee for thy great glory." Very apparent in both Catholic and Protestant worship is the desire to glorify the name of God by means of worship.

Another prominent end might be called instruction as seen in the great care taken for commemoration in orderly fashion of the works of God, both those recorded in the Bible and those manifested ever since the first century in the lives of the saints. Certainly there are elements of the glorification of God in the Church calendar. But one can also detect an effort to educate both clergy and laity in the fullness of celebration. Likewise, the effort made in using the arts to communicate the history of salvation from creation to the day of judgment is a vivid means of communicating Christian doctrine.

Through various complex developments, a characteristic late medieval belief was that the mass could be offered to procure various intentions. The consequence was that the mass could be conceived of as offered in order to use Christ's work to secure one's desires. The extreme case would be to secure the death of someone, an intention specifically forbidden in A.D. 694. More common would be the remedy of ills in this life or speeding the passage through purgatory in the next. All this implied, of course, that worship was being treated as something done to acquire merit. One could sanction worship because it conferred merit upon the worshiper. An excessive emphasis on this purpose lies behind Luther railing against misuse of the mass as a "place of merchandise."[6] Luther feared the mass had been conceived too narrowly as a sacrifice that man offered to God instead of something offered by God to man. Disagreement over this particular end sought in worship was one of the forces that gave vigor to the Reformation. Today Roman Catholics would be less inclined to speak of the grace of the sacraments in juridical terms, and the legalism that scandalized Luther might be pushed aside in favor of more biblical and personal concepts.

The Reformers found some of the ends sought in medieval worship very repugnant. Luther was especially forceful in denying that the worship of God brought merit, and most of the other Reformers agreed with his attitude completely. In Luther's writing the benefits of worship receive considerable attention. Worship is frequently described as conveying the promises of God. This happens

[6] "The Babylonian Captivity of the Church," *Works of Martin Luther* (Philadelphia: Muhlenberg Press, 1943), II, 194.

especially through the preaching of God's Word and it is no accident that preaching became so important for Luther that he could write: "The chief and greatest aim of any Service is to preach and teach God's Word."[7] Emphasis on receiving the benefits of God's promises figures prominently in Calvin's writings too. Both Luther and Calvin stress our need for "partaking of all his [Christ's] benefits" received through the signs of the promises that God "accommodating himself to our capacity" has provided in worship.

Other less commendable ends sought in worship appeared in the tendency to make worship a means of teaching theological doctrines, even to the point of including disputes in the consecration prayer of the Church of England. More appropriate benefits sought in the Lord's Supper included the desire to "receive and feed upon Christ crucified" (*Westminster Confession*), taking the "Sacrament to your comfort" (1549 *Book of Common Prayer*), or Wesley's description of it as "a mercy to man" and a "converting ordinance."

In the nineteenth and twentieth centuries other purposes became prominent, in addition to the ancient ones of the glorification of God, the expression of gratitude to Him, and hearing and receiving His promises. Many varying purposes sought in worship come to light in the expression "getting something out of it." More often than not, behind this phrase lies a longing for cosmic stability, a recharging of spiritual batteries by gaining a Browning-like assurance ("God's in His heaven—All's right with the world!"). Characteristic of such motivations for worship seem to be the psychologically beneficial effects on the

[7]"The German Mass," *Liturgies of the Western Church*, edited by Bard Thompson (Cleveland: Meridian Books, 1961), p. 129.

worshiper, particularly in giving him a sense of security in a changing world. One could label these justifications for worship as therapeutic.

It is not so simple to evaluate motivations for worship that revolve around the accomplishing of some purpose. Some ends are a great deal more theologically satisfactory than others. Worship as directed to the glorification of God is hardly comparable to worship performed because "the family that prays together stays together," as the advertising media have assured us. One must admit the patent ambiguity of the latter assertion and recognize that the motivation is a limited one, directed to insuring the stability of a small group. Some ends are obviously selfish and introverted; others express "benevolence to being in general,"[8] i.e. God, in the fullest way.

We do not condemn the intent to accomplish certain ends as insufficient motivation for worship. But there is a great deal of ambiguity about such incentives to worship. One must examine individually each purpose advocated. Some ends will seem theologically justifiable as accurately reflecting man's relation to God. Others may miss the mark widely by not corresponding to the way God relates to man. Such would seem to be the case with some of the more common ends that promote worship largely as a means of creating a deceptive sense of adjustment and security.

III

It is far from possible to do complete justice to the various motivations for worship by forcing them to fit the cate-

[8]Jonathan Edwards, *The Nature of True Virtue* (Ann Arbor: University of Michigan Press, 1960), p. 3.

gories of doing one's duty or accomplishing some good. Certainly some expressions of why we worship fit one or the other of these classifications quite well. But human motivations are much too rich and complex to be comprehended entirely by either category.

We have not yet given an adequate answer to our question: "Why worship?" There is a spontaneous quality about worship that transcends the more deliberate sense of doing right or accomplishing good. Luther expressed this aspect precisely in his simple statement: "For to have God is to worship God."[9] There is an inevitable quality about worship that the motivations we have mentioned fail to suggest.

I would like to suggest that the most adequate and comprehensive way for understanding the motivation to worship is by regarding it as a response, a response to what has happened and is happening to us. Here we may utilize some concepts developed by H. Richard Niebuhr in his discussion of the ethics of the fitting. As Niebuhr states with regard to ethics, the motivation of response reflects "the understanding of ourselves as responsive beings, who in all our actions answer to action upon us in accordance with our interpretation of such action."[10] This is no simple definition! But it does have some real advantages. It comprehends the sense of doing what is right, as when one responds by worshiping because he thinks it is demanded of him. And it includes worship performed in order to achieve some purpose such as showing gratitude. And response, the doing of what is fitting, does justice to the non-analytic, the spontaneous aspect of our will to worship.

[9]*Martin Luthers Werke, Tischreden* (Weimar: Hermann Bohlaus Nachfolge, 1919), V, 47.

[10]*The Responsible Self* (New York: Harper & Row, 1963), p. 57.

Analyzing motivations in terms of response is particularly useful in the case of worship, since many of the forms and expressions used in worship refer specifically to the prior actions of God. Closely linked in worship are the commemoration of the actions of God and the response of praise and thanksgiving for them. In this sense it is not only possible but necessary to speak of worship as doing that which seems fitting.

Worship when seen as motivated by response reflects an understanding of the first actor as divine. We act, as Niebuhr says, in "answer to action upon us." We respond because of our understanding of the ways in which God's activity impinges upon us through the persons and situations of our daily life. In worship, we respond, not to the proximate, that nearest to us, but to the ultimate, God, whom we see working through the then and there of the past and the here and now of the present. We respond to God, and worship is the most obvious and natural form for such response. Praise based on response is the keynote of Christian (and Jewish) worship, as indicated in Psalm 150: "Praise him for his mighty deeds; praise him according to his exceeding greatness!"

Before we settle too readily for responding to God's activity as the most adequate means of understanding the motivation to worship, we must remember that there is another clause in Niebuhr's definition of the ethics of the fitting. The response is "in accordance with our interpretation of such action." Worship is not just a response to God's actions but to our "*interpretation*" of the questions " 'What is going on?' or 'What is being done to me?' "[11] The response has a very personal element, since it is determined by my understanding of what is happening to

[11]Ibid. p. 63.

myself. Worship is one form by which we respond to the way we interpret God's activity in the world about us. Much of our discussion in this book will revolve around the twin themes of our awareness of what is going on about us and the way we respond to this interpretation of reality.

This means we must raise basic questions concerning our understanding of how God relates to men in order to discuss worship further. We must discuss our interpretations of human history, of the orders of creation, and of the structures of human society. Obviously these are complex matters, but without scanning them we can hardly hope to gain insight into the nature of Christian worship. No doubt the basic problem of worship is the problem of how one understands the nature of reality, in technical terms the question of ontology (the nature of being).

Our question: "Why worship?" is best answered by considering the primary motivation as the attempt to make our own fitting response to our understanding of what God is doing in the world. There are times when other motivations stand out with considerable clarity, but the motivation of response seems to be the most fundamental reason for worshiping.

II

THE FORMS AND SUBSTANCE OF WORSHIP

The most obvious fact about public worship is that it is a social act. Public worship is done together as an act of the assembled Christian community and is perhaps best described as common worship. The very social nature of common worship makes it the opposite of Plotinus' "flight of the alone to the alone."[1] Common worship is perhaps the most intensely social act of the Christian community.

All social acts need forms in order to avoid chaos and confusion. One has only to reflect upon how carefully formalized a family meal is to realize how utterly dependent we are upon the use of established forms. The business meeting of any club or organization follows recognized rules of order. Otherwise it would be most difficult to transact business. Any sport is played by well-established rules of the game. One could hardly play baseball if there were not prior agreement that three strikes put a player out and that three outs retire a team. Without these forms only confusion would result.

Therefore it is not at all surprising that worship needs set forms. If the congregation is to worship in common

[1]*Enneads,* VI, ix, 11.

there must be established forms so that worship can be done together. Even so-called free forms of worship depend upon an accustomed form of worship. This should not be confused with a formal spirit or atmosphere. Forms may be used in an informal way as in the worship of the East Harlem Protestant Parish, where the forms are fixed but the spirit is informal. The use of forms is inevitable, but the spirit in which they are used can be informal or formal. One does not escape dependence upon forms even in Quaker worship.

The forms used in common worship can be summarized under three headings: structure, words, and actions. Any service of worship needs a basic structure in order that the sequence may be obvious to all. One could hardly expect worship to be a social act if some were singing while others were listening to preaching. Structure is as necessary as the order of business is in a club meeting. Christian worship is largely verbal. A major portion of Christian worship revolves around the spoken word. This should not be strange in a religion which makes the Word its dominant symbol. Even Quaker worship relies heavily on words as a basic form. In addition worship makes use of actions or movements. As we shall see, actions are a basic mode of communication and expression. The rubrics are often as important as the texts. Even the postures of the congregation are significant.

Forms, however, are relative to time and place, varying to some degree from culture to culture. Though forms are necessary and important, the substance of worship is even more significant. By substance we mean that which the forms communicate and express, the meaning, the inner existential quality of worship. Compared with the substance of worship, forms are indeed only as "sounding brass, or a tinkling cymbal" (KJV). The brass and cymbal serve a real purpose but only to express the substance of worship. Forms and substance, of course, cannot be absolutely distinguished in worship any more than in art. But just as we do talk about technique and subject matter in painting, though they are finally inseparable, so we may take the risk of speaking of forms and substance separately with regard to worship.

Unfortunately, most scholarship has concentrated on the forms of worship. It is possible to compare various forms, to trace their ancestry back into New Testament times and beyond, to group them into families, and to adapt them for contemporary use. But this is only to touch upon the husk of worship and to miss its kernel. To discuss the substance of worship is much more difficult and has usually been avoided in recent scholarship. The historians have done well in chronicling and analyzing the forms of worship. But the exploration of the substance of worship, more properly the theologian's task, has been relatively ignored. In contrast to the impressive studies of ethics, Protestant theologians have done little to provide a contemporary theology of worship. For the most part, the subject has been ignored or only briefly treated in short articles or occasional chapters.

The study of worship as an academic discipline has been almost confined to historical research. It may well be that the study of worship will have to be saved from the historians just as they once saved it from the psychologists. And the responsibility would seem to rest with the theologians whose work is so basic to every other area of the Church's life. A close partnership between theology and preaching has developed in our time but this liaison seems to be lacking when it comes to the other aspects of worship, particularly the orderly and systematic study of the substance of worship itself.

This is a difficult and complex area of investigation. We are presenting here only a preliminary exploration in hopes of opening up the basic questions and showing some of the areas which demand attention.

I

What then is the substance of worship? It is almost to ask: "What is worship?" There are few words harder to define than worship. Merely to describe the forms of worship will not do. Simply to reiterate the derivation of our English term worship (from the Old English *weorth,* worthy and *scipe,* ship) does not help much more.

The method we will take in discussing the substance of worship is that of risking a definition and then explaining the definition. In briefest terms the definition is this: Worship is the act of standing outside of our normal consciousness in order to become aware of God and to respond to him. Each part of this definition will need our attention.

Although it has a great deal of continuity with the rest of life (as we shall see below), worship also involves an element of discontinuity. Worship involves a break from our normal consciousness. It means a stepping aside from normal life in order to perceive it in a deeper and more significant way. One cannot appreciate the full continuity of worship and the rest of life without this sense of standing outside of our usual consciousness in order to encounter reality in greater depth. The problem is not that "the world is too much with us" but that we do not take seriously enough the necessity of a temporary withdrawal from the world in worship in order to understand the true nature of life. As we shall argue, worship is a very worldly activity but genuine worldliness is made possible only through the depth in which worship makes us encounter the world.

Worship as a temporary standing aside is not flight from the world but a means of being with the world and oneself at a deeper level. The standing aside is only a brief separation from our superficial consciousness in order to plumb the depths of life in a fashion we fail to do otherwise. It is to treat both God and His world with the seriousness they deserve.

There are two aspects to standing outside of one's usual consciousness: reconsideration of being and the response to it. In what ways does worship involve reconsideration? In this moment of seeking a deeper level of being one encounters the divine activity in various ways. It brings insight into what one already knows but does not keep in mind. God is no more present to the worshiper than to one not worshiping. But in worship we become aware of that which is. One can speak of this as reconsideration or recollection since it is not the discovery of new knowledge, "no sudden rending of the veil of clay," but a return to what one has really known in the past and yet repeatedly forgotten.

Reconsideration involves the realization that God acts in our midst. It is partly the sense among those gathered together that God is with them. But it is also the realization that God is acting for those not gathered together in His name. In worship one becomes aware of the dependence of all men upon God's actions. As he worships one sees the world about him as the scene of what God is doing. This is no new discovery but one that vanishes easily from the mind until reconsidered in worship. One knows that the world depends upon God acting for it, and yet one does not know it until he recollects it in worship.

One of the most important aspects of this recollection is that worship consists largely in the commemoration of acts that the Christian community has isolated as revealing the nature of God's work. The life and death of Jesus Christ stand out above all else as the key disclosure of God acting in human history. One knows that God is working in the present largely because of the witness to His activity in the past. It is for this reason that a major portion of almost any service of Christian worship is a rehearsal of the acts of God narrated in Scripture. Over the centuries various ways have been developed for recalling in our worship the cycle of biblical events, especially those recorded in the gospels. In the continued reconsideration of these past events the worshiper makes his own once again that on which his knowledge of God is based.

In worship one reconsiders his relation to the world about him. The orders of creation reveal their true character as agencies of divine origin and sustenance. Man in his social nature as a member of society is seen as he is. The state, the powers of organized man to do business, to educate, to protect himself, and so forth, stand out in their true character as created structures. We are constantly aware of these aspects of life, but rarely, except in worship, do we become conscious of them in their true character as parts of God's creating activity.

In worship one sees his neighbor in God, so that he reconsiders his relationship to those about him. When confronted with God one realizes his responsibility to his neighbor. The vertical relationship immediately implies a horizontal one. This is especially true in the dynamics of public worship where the mutual witness of other Christians is so obvious. The time of reconsideration re-establishes one's true relationship to his neighbor—that of fellow servants called upon to serve each other.

The time of reconsideration brings one to a deeper understanding of himself. In worship one comes to act out what one really is, God's creature, reflecting his Creator's image, having dominion over God's world. At the same time, he is a sinner to whom Christ has imputed His righteousness. One already knows this. But he appropriates it anew in reconsidering the nature of his true being during worship. In confession one realizes anew his sin but in absolution knows himself as standing under forgiveness instead of judgment. In offering his "sacrifice of praise and thanksgiving" one acknowledges his dependency upon God and his creaturehood.

To summarize: In standing outside of his normal consciousness and reconsidering, one acknowledges the nature of God and all being. In this time of reconsideration the true nature of existence again becomes apparent. One sees himself in relation to God, to the world about himself, and to himself, as these things really are. Thus worship is, in a sense, an encounter with reality.

But one cannot understand worship as reconsideration alone. Reconsideration implies a "therefore." This being so, therefore I respond. The other half of worship is that of response. One responds to that which he has found to be true and significant in the nature of being.

Here too worship is both intensely corporate and intensely personal. One responds with the assembled group, but one is also expressing the significance of what has been recollected for himself. Although worship is a common witness, it is at the same time an intensely personal witness. The self does not disappear in common worship; it is enabled to be itself with greater profundity. The witness of others enables us to respond to what has significance for our own life.

The basic character of response in Christian worship is that of praise. One rejoices and gives thanks for what God has done, particularly for the Christ event. One gives praise for what one discovers in the world, his neighbor, and himself. And one praises God in the hope of His continuing creative activity. The salient feature of praise is that it is a response based upon the activity of God, not on ourselves. Due to a one-sided distortion of the substance of worship in Western Christianity, many of our forms concentrate upon man's sinfulness. But this is somewhat irrelevant. True, one rediscovers himself as sinner in worship, but if that were all it would hardly be worth pursuing. The important thing in worship is that one sees God as all in all. Hence one's response is not to his own sinfulness but to the God who died for sinners. To go to church to tell God what sinners we are (even with a bit of pride for being such "miserable offenders") is to miss the point. It is rather like telling a famous surgeon about the tonsillectomy we once had.

Praise, as Eastern Christians know full well, is the basic and inevitable response to awareness of the activity of God. It is no wonder that the Psalter is the great hymn book of the Christian Church and has been such from the days of the early Church. Many hymns, both ancient and modern, are reflections of the psalms and their constant reiteration of praise to God. Many of the psalms and hymns used by the Church contain both recitals of and praise for what God has done, is doing, and promises to do. Frequently the essence of worship is summed up in a single psalm: recollection and response. The writer of Psalm 8 reflects: "When I look at thy heavens, the work of thy fingers" and then goes on to exclaim, "How majestic is thy name in all the earth!" The popularity of the psalms is no accident; they ring true to the Christian understanding of worship. For the most part the psalms do not praise God for abstract qualities but for what He has done and what He is doing. The divine activity is praised.

Granted the primacy of praise, there are other elements of response in worship which are important though to lesser degrees. Our self-understanding as sinners, reconsidered in worship, inevitably leads to penitence. Our needs are voiced as petitions and the needs of others as intercessions. The awareness of what God has done for us leads us to offer ourselves to Him. The "sacrifice of praise and thanksgiving," after all, is only a symbol of the offering of our total beings. That was done for me, therefore I wish to do this in return. It is not an automatic *quid pro quo,* but a sense of joyful response to serve that which is Ultimate by serving that which is proximate, my neighbor. Worship makes us respond beyond the narrow hour that circumscribes our gathering.

There occur some practical problems in the life of the Church with regard to the elements of reconsideration and response. Two of these need our immediate attention: the problem of Christian education and that of our inhibitions with regard to response. We will survey these areas briefly.

The problem of the relation between Christian education and worship is a most complex one to which insufficient attention has been given. Perhaps symptomatic of this is that hardly ever does the design of church buildings give any indication of a meaningful relationship between the facilities for worship and those for education. Yet the question is an important one: just what is the relation between worship and education? We have stated that worship is a reconsideration in depth of what one already knows. This would indicate that worship is not primarily an educational activity in the sense of learning new material, though it is in the sense of appropriating in greater depth what one already knows. Both education and worship, therefore, share in the process of Christian formation.

Becoming a Christian is not simply a matter of acquiring the necessary information, as might be the case in becoming a licensed electrician. It is a matter of formation in which one's stance on life, his style of living, becomes changed. Formation or nurture is the gradual and often imperceptible change of one's being. The biological definition of nurture as "the sum of the influences modifying the expression of the genetic potentialities of an organism" (Webster's Third) is a close parallel to our present use of these terms. One can easily see that formation is more than a matter of learning new information about Christian doctrine, history, or ethics. Formation is a process in which one's being undergoes a change. In the terms of Jonathan Edwards, one's "strongest motive"[2] is changed. This means worship, along with education and other activities of the Church, changes one's future. It is no sudden change but a continual formation of our being.

Sometimes questions are raised about the temporal sequence of worship and Christian education. It is occa-

[2] *Freedom of the Will*, edited by Paul Ramsey (New Haven: Yale University Press, 1957), p. 141.

sionally asked: "Which comes first, worship or Christian education?" It must be remembered that both activities contribute to changing one's mental attitudes. Christian education would seem to create an attitude whereby worship becomes inevitable. One would not only learn how to worship but also undergo a change so that worship would seem desirable to him. Worship, on the other hand, raises questions of a theological nature that demand discussion and clarification. Which comes first then, worship or education?

It may be said that worship is the prior activity on the grounds that worship plays such a major role in formation and does impart a considerable amount of information, especially biblical. There is no denying that much of worship, particularly the reading of Scripture and preaching, has an obvious didactic aspect. Furthermore one becomes aware of areas of necessary inquiry by the reconsideration of being that worship entails.

On the other hand it may be said that one has little to reconsider in depth until his mind has been formed in some extent by education. This would seem to reflect the practice of the early Church, which restricted attendance of catechumens (those receiving preliminary instructions) to the service of the Word only, the first half of holy communion. Only when well grounded in the faith and baptized were they allowed to remain for the entire service. One of the strongest criticisms of the current practice of walk-in Church membership (receiving into membership the stranger who walks down the aisle on Sunday morning) is that some kind of catechumenate would seem to be necessary before Christian worship or any Christian practices can mean much more than sentimental quaintness. For better or for worse, there is a Christian vocabulary, and mastering this would seem to be a prerequisite for worship.

To both these positions it may be answered that worship and education belong together, that a strict time sequence is not desirable, though possibly some prior education is generally preferable. It is indeed difficult in American society for any educated person to be a thorough pagan. The forms of our society often communicate the outer shell of Christianity. Thus rarely does one approach Christianity as a complete outsider. On the other hand, the amount of education is usually fragmentary and superficial. Christian education is a necessary part of one's formation as a Christian and it never ends. Thus one cannot say: "Wait until you have finished your Christian education in order to worship." For then one would never be ready. In addition, one may see in many a church the tendency for education to monopolize the process of formation. Adult Sunday School classes, especially those with popular teachers, tend to become small churches within the congregation and for many class members worship seems unnecessary.

Worship and education go together. Both are parts of the same process of formation. The dispassionate objectifying of God and the theological questioning present in the best of Christian education need the acts of reconsideration and response present in worship. But worship, particularly in order to make the element of reconsideration as true to being as possible, needs the intellectual demands of Christian education. Both belong together and suffer when separated.

The problems with regard to response are of a quite different nature. They seem to stem largely from the overdeveloped self-consciousness so typical of middle-class

Christians. One may wish to express his response with fervor, but increasingly the various modes of expression have been stifled by self-consciousness. Good taste has become the supreme arbiter of our lives. Any enthusiastic response has been banished in the average middle-class church and many elements of response have been handed over to the professional worshipers, the ministers and choir members. One of the most marked characteristics of the average middle-class church in America, Protestant or Catholic, is the inhibition that prevents fervent response.

It was not so a generation or more ago when the elements of response were much more obvious. Certainly the fervent "amen" during the sermon and prayers was an excellent means of sharing in the Word. But it failed to conform to a starched notion of dignity and we were embarrassed out of it. The zealous "hallelujah" could hardly survive the same scrutiny. With worship becoming more and more polite, the forms expressive of response have become limited and often today are participated in so timidly that people are apt to turn and stare at anyone who sings a hymn as if he meant it. Self-consciousness may have changed our worship more than any theological shift.

There is no easy remedy for this situation. But one can learn from others not yet afflicted by the same deadening inhibitions. The worship of the Negro churches and pentecostal groups comes most quickly to mind. It is not impossible that the renewal of Christian worship may come from the Negro churches. One of the unsuspected benefits of integration is in fulfilling our need of each other's understanding of worship. The substance of worship is sometimes more obvious in the worship of Negro and pentecostal churches than elsewhere. There the standing aside from daily life, the reconsideration of its meaning, and the response are certainly obvious. One can hardly fail to be impressed with the difference between the staid dignified service of the established churches and that of our Negro churches with their foot-tapping music, their occasional exclamations of great joy, and the excitement of their worship.

It is no accident that the modern freedom movement is the most creative liturgical force in America today. Who can sing and sway, chanting: "Freedom, freedom, freedom" without seeing the parallels with Christian worship? It is high time we looked more seriously at what can be learned from the worship of Negro Christians.

How do we overcome our inhibitions and recover warmth and spontaneity? How do you teach naïveté? It is perhaps the only thing you cannot teach. And even if the kingdom of heaven is like a little child, one cannot reverse the process of physical growth. We have lost our innocence and cannot duplicate the forms that now express worship in Negro and pentecostal churches so successfully, or even those forms our grandfathers used. Nevertheless, it is essential to find a way to prevent our self-consciousness from completely inhibiting any really expressive response in our worship. Can we shed our dignity when it interferes with warmth and spontaneity in worship? The youth who have shown more interest in jazz masses and folk masses are less fearful of genuine expression than many of their parents. Certainly here is direct evidence of the importance of forms.

Some forms are much more successful than others in expressing response. Music has a peculiar power to allow one to stand outside of his normal means of articulation and to communicate at a deeper level. There is all the difference in the world between a spoken service and one sung. This is why congregational singing is so important in worship, and why a lack of singing often means a passive and indifferent congregation. Bits of dialogue and responses can be good opportunities for expressive participation. The recovery of the Psalter is a most encouraging sign in Christian worship today. Here one finds his own response frequently and forcibly rendered in words. Various actions, such as going forward to receive the sacrament at holy communion, can also be highly successful vehicles of manifesting our involvement in worship. On the negative side are those elements of worship that keep the congregation passive: too much choral music, too many musical interludes, and clerical monopolizing of prayer. The challenge before us is to make the most of those forms that give the whole congregation an opportunity to express its response in worship and to avoid those elements that discourage this.

Even more important than the form of worship, however, is its substance. We have depicted it as the coming to awareness of, and the response to, God. We must constantly remind ourselves that substance is primary; forms are simply containers for the substance of worship. The appearance of the containers may change or they may even be disposable. But the packaging is what one usually sees, and we shall spend most of our time discussing forms. Let us remember that the forms used for worship should always be evaluated with respect to their ability to express the substance of worship.

II

Having said this, we must remember that forms are absolutely essential for any kind of public worship. We must, then, examine forms a bit more closely and shall do this following the three patterns mentioned previously: structure, words, and actions.

By structure we mean the sequence of the various elements that comprise the service of worship. How important is the structure of a service? It is possible that it has received too much attention in our time. The shape of the liturgy is important, but it can also become a subtle form of idolatry in itself. Luther's statement to the effect that those who are already Christian could dispense with set forms altogether, though they abide by them out of love to their neighbor, has an element of truth in it.[3] One can give too much attention to structure in which case it becomes idolatrous.

One of the dangers is in thinking that there is such a thing as correctness in structure. Undoubtedly some structures are inadequate since they misrepresent Christian doctrines. But to assume that there is a correct structure, discovered either through historical study or rationalization is wrong. One hears of a minister who noticed that every time he brought the structure of his service closer to his ideal there were fewer people present, and finally concluded that when he had perfected it there might be no one there at all. Those who find a correct form by referring to history usually do it at the cost of gross oversimplification. To be sure, there can be found a number of areas in which something of a historical consensus is possible, and yet when one pushes into details there is likely to be conflicting evidence. This is not to say that history should be taken lightly. It should be taken very seriously, but not as if it would divulge some correct ideal structure. Though most of our basic structures congealed

[3]B. Thompson (ed), "The German Mass," *Liturgies of the Western Church,* p. 124.

somewhere between the second and sixth centuries, changes have continually occurred since then. The achievement of uniformity was a mistaken ideal of the sixteenth century, made possible by the invention of printing. It can exist only by ignoring all cultural differences between nations and groups within nations, a price too great to pay for uniformity.

One would do well to abide by the tradition of his own part of the Church. For any deviation the burden of proof is upon the person making the change. But sometimes change is necessary and should be carried out. Unfortunately those churches that have given the minister the most freedom in the ordering of worship have also done the least to educate him in this area. It is vital to study the history of Christian worship but one should not have any naïve expectation of finding a correct structure. A correct structure in worship is just as elusive as a correct response in ethics.

The other temptation is to rationalize the existing structure of worship. Most of those who write with this approach find that worship is divided into three, four, five, or more acts. They then proceed to set forth a rationale for the sequence they prefer. All these rationalizations are *ex post facto*, for they have been applied to inherited structures. Such an effort always requires a bit of imagination. Christian worship is not a particularly tidy affair. Its strength has been in adequately reflecting the nature of God and the experiences of men, and these are matters hardly contained within neat formulas. These matters are not susceptible to any simple rationalization. Those things that have survived in Christian worship have done so because of their adequacy, not because they fitted any pattern.

When one looks at most of the traditional services of worship he finds they have elements of anachronism and discontinuity that cannot be rationalized away. Episcopal and Methodist communion services contain the words "draw near" but at a point at which people ceased to draw near two and a half centuries ago. On what basis does one rationalize the location of the Lord's Prayer in a morning order of worship? Would it not fit in many schemes with equal ease or lack of it? Such efforts to systematize worship are likely to force it into individualistic limits and to make us forget that the traditional forms of worship are as unsystematic as life itself.

A common sport in recent years has been that of trying to systematize the Christian year. The Christian year does not fit into any rational scheme. It retains those days and seasons that have proved themselves to be of value over the centuries in representing God's actions and helping men appropriate them. But the Christian year is the product of slow evolution and not of systematic development. Occasional efforts have been made to tidy up the commemoration of the saints but not the seasons. The Christian year has strength because it has rung true to human experience. Efforts to give it a trinitarian pattern or any other miss this point.

One may be tempted to rationalize worship in order to explain or interpret it to others. When this is done by categorizing portions of the service through headings in the church bulletin or otherwise it is apt to make worship even more self-conscious. Such a clinical approach may be necessary in lecturing and writing about worship just as medical students find it necessary to dissect a corpse. But the corpse should never be mistaken for the living tissue of worship.

Such attempts run into necessary oversimplifications. One will be tempted to designate certain acts as praise and others as proclamation and so forth. But actually every act of worship is an act of praise and in every act the gospel is proclaimed. I praise God by listening to His word just as I praise Him in saying the psalms. The gospel is proclaimed in the fact that I confess and am forgiven just as in preaching. Worship is one whole loaf no matter how many ways one slices it. It might be more helpful instead of schematizing worship to approach the service as a whole and then to note the degree to which each act reflects reconsideration and response. Each act is a part of the whole structure and derives its significance from that, not from being a part of a rationalized order.

It may sound as if the structure of worship is a matter of indifference. That is not the case. But the temptations to find a correct structure by plunging into history or by creating one's own rationalization should be resisted. The value of structure is in preserving as fully as possible the Christian understanding of God's nature and doing justice to the experience of life as men live it. Some structures are so narrowly conceived that they fail to do this. For example, a service that ignores the fact that man is a sinner and that God forgives the penitent would seem to be deficient. Structure then is important in reflecting an adequate theology. Most of the major traditions are adequate here simply because they have reflected the experiences of Christians over a wide span of time. One would do well to take them seriously but not uncritically. The best procedure, then, would seem to be that of not departing from an inherited tradition except for sound theological reasons and then not to attempt an overly rationalized and systematized structure.

The use of words in worship is of utmost importance to the Christian. Other religions may be able to worship without words, but Christianity can hardly be mute. Since the verbal nature of worship is so prominent, it is not surprising that numerous problems arise with regard to the use of words in worship. We shall outline briefly the chief problems.

It does not take much reflection to realize that words are used in a different fashion in worship than they are elsewhere. In worship we play a different word game than in theological talk. In both instances we use myths and symbols to communicate our meaning. But theology employs the categories of modern knowledge to interpret myths. The language of myths is used but it is a "broken myth." This becomes particularly apparent in the effort to demythologize, that is, to divest the understanding of God's actions of the first century A.D. of the thought forms and symbols meaningful in that time but not in ours.

Worship uses myths and symbols in a more literal fashion. One does not demythologize in worshiping. Worship takes short cuts, theology cannot. The myths and symbols are used in their traditional way, many of them hardly changed since biblical times. Liberal-critical theologians and fundamentalists unite in using the language of the Apostles' Creed in worship. But as theological disputants they use the same words quite differently than they do as worshipers. An important part of almost any type of worship is the reading of the Scriptures. Here from the myth of creation to the myth of the last judgment the thought forms are those of early civilizations. The symbols used in talking about God as king or shepherd reflect past ages. If one analyzes the language of any service of worship it will be found to be filled with symbolic language that reveals its ancient origin. "Lost sheep," "sitteth at the right hand of God," "as it was in the beginning," all of these and many more are word pictures from bygone days. We do not talk this way any more.

Why do we use such symbols in worship? This suggests a closer view of the function of a religious symbol. A religious symbol is a means of expressing the ultimate by means of the proximate. One uses a word of known meaning, such as father or fatherhood, to approximate our understanding of that which transcends any meaning we give to it. We speak of God as Father or of the Fatherhood of God. Now we know that this is not an adequate definition of God's being, but it is one of the best ways of describing our understanding of man's dependence, obedience, and trust in God. The symbol taken from our daily experience of fatherhood becomes an analogy of the Divine Being. That which transcends language nevertheless can be approximated by the use of a common symbol.

Not all words can serve as symbols in this way. The association is not an accidental one. Symbols have their power because they participate in some way in the reality to which they refer.[4] The power of a word like Father when applied to God is that our heavenly Father has some of the aspects of an earthly father. God as king represents some of the qualities we apply to earthly kingship: power, majesty, and absolute sovereignty. On the other hand, arbitrary associations do not work this way. As a result many people were shocked to see Jesus symbolized by a clown in a recent movie (*The Parable*), even though sensitively done. Physical symbols such as bread and wine have their particular power because they have so much in common with body and blood. They also have power

[4]Paul Tillich, *Dynamics of Faith* (New York: Harper & Row, 1957), p. 42.

because of long association. Thus we have a clue to another characteristic of symbols; they derive much of their power from long association.

It is a perfectly legitimate question to ask whether the extensive use of myth and symbol in Christian worship is justified or not. If theology can break the myth, why does not worship do so too? Even further, why not jettison myths and symbols stained with the ancient past, since they are hard for modern man to comprehend and sometimes offensive to our contemporaries?

One does not seem to have such an alternative. It is necessary to use symbols and myths to express our worship. Tillich reminds us that only symbols can express our relationship to that which is ultimate.[5] No other form of expression seems to be available. There seems to be no way of avoiding symbolic expressions in worship any more than in other ways of communicating in depth. The heart has little to do with love but remains a symbolic representation of that which is exceedingly difficult to express otherwise. If one were to eliminate all the ancient symbols in worship, he would almost necessarily have to replace them with new ones. Symbolic language seems to be a necessity for expressing worship.

However, this is not to solve our problem by any means. Symbols or language are not static matters. It is entirely possible that a symbol that once had a great deal of power can lose it altogether. The visual symbol of the peacock means little to the Christian of today except perhaps as signifying color television. The pomegranate has even less significance. Yet both of these once said "resurrection" to early Christians. Symbols die and might just as well be given a decent Christian burial. To try to revive a dead

[5]Ibid. p. 53.

symbol is almost impossible. To speak of Christ as priest, a biblical symbol, is probably not to speak to modern man. Possibly the same is true of the language of sacrifice, though to our loss. If the symbols are dead we must admit the fact and eliminate them.

The replacement of symbols, however, is not so easily done. Symbols do not grow simply out of taking thought, springing forth full-grown like Venus. They sneak up on us. Suddenly the things we have been doing in worship appear to us as symbols though they were never intended as such. In such a fashion, the garments worn by nuns, Catholic priests, and Protestant ministers were once ordinary fashionable dress but in the course of time became hallowed, gradually coming to have more than purely utilitarian functions. They are now recognized as symbols, though never intended as such originally.

We must let old symbols die but we cannot consciously create new ones. Is there any way out of this situation, or are we left with an ever decreasing number of verbal and visual symbols? Fortunately new symbols are undoubtedly developing before our eyes without our being completely conscious of them. In the meantime we have a great variety of symbols which despite their time-stained quality seem to have an amazing vitality. Anyone who has lived on a sheep ranch knows how wonderfully graphic are the tremendous variety of biblical images that revolve around sheep-herding. But most people today have never taken a lamb to the slaughter or gone in search of a lost sheep. In fact in many cities today there are people who have never seen a sheep and might be more terrified than a ewe itself if confronted with one.

Yet one can hardly discard such central biblical symbols as the Good Shepherd or the lamb led to the slaughter.

Fortunately these images, though archaic, do still have considerable power to communicate reality. The same is true of the symbols of kingship, though the personal associations here are even more remote than with sheep. Indeed some of these ancient symbols still have an amazing power to communicate even though the immediate reference is obsolete. Part of the power of the biblical symbols may very well come from the fact that most of the symbols are not primarily religious ones but taken from ordinary life, politics, farming, and so forth. Some such as those referring to the body are never likely to grow obsolete. Others such as those clustering around blood may have less power today than when carcasses hung in every marketplace. One would hesitate today to speak of a "fountain filled with blood." But the symbols of blood retain a great deal of power even though blood may less obviously represent the life of creatures than it once did.

We actually have more potent symbols available than we perhaps realize, largely due to the worldly language of the Bible. The religious symbols such as the priestly ones seem to have been more perishable than the others. We have many more worldly symbols than we manage to use and they very well may communicate better than we are willing to concede.

One other problem involving words demands attention even if briefly. This is the obsolescence of words and is a major problem in worship. Many people are vaguely unhappy about "vouchsafeth" and "beseech" and the type of language that they represent. Most of these terms are relics of Elizabethan English. It seems to be mostly the verbs that are offensive, though problems are raised by the pronouns "thee" and "thou." What shall we do with obsolete language?

Two obvious courses suggest themselves. One of these is simply to retain the language no matter how obsolete, and so Episcopalians go on with their promise to "plight thee my troth." The other extreme seems to be that of introducing contemporary language, as in one Methodist church where the minister, tiring of the biblical, "The Lord be with you," substituted a breezy "Hi there!" The problem of the first course is that of complete incomprehension. The problem of the second is that so many such attempts tend to be comical. One is more inclined to laugh than anything else.

Part of the problem is that we have many private languages in a pluralistic society. I never understand the people who fix my car. I don't do too much better with doctors, though at least I can identify the parts in question. Presumably doctors can speak to each other without problems of communication. Perhaps we succeed better in using a common language in worship than we are willing to admit. It may well be that the slow evolution of the language of worship is a factor in making it common, whereas rapid change might render it even more an exclusive jargon of the initiated. The advertising media have shown us that reiteration is an effective way of learning even completely nonsensical gibberish. If repetition can persuade us to put a tiger in our tank, the same method may help us put a shepherd in our psalm.

There seems to be a natural conservatism with regard to the language of worship. Phrases tend to become hallowed by our growing accustomed to them. People are generally conservative when it comes to worship and this is not necessarily a mistaken instinct. Most likely the answer is the same as with symbols; some words should be allowed to die but a wholesale slaughter is not called for. Moderation seems to make more sense; more contemporary verbs, perhaps, but toleration of thee's and thou's if necessary. And even these may not be necessary much longer. "And with thy spirit" makes less sense than "and with you too." The second form comes closer to the original meaning (Ruth 2:4) than the accustomed form. Another reason for the retention of traditional language is not conservatism but the instinct to reflect the otherness of God by using forms of address more dignified and elevated than one ordinarily uses. In the same way a lover may use a more exalted language than he normally employs.

The wisest course with regard to language would seem to be moderate progression. Obsolete phrases can be discarded but there seems to be little real advantage in using language that is really "with it." Chances are that in a few years it won't be anyhow! The latest thing soon becomes the dreariest thing. Most newly concocted liturgical language seems more esoteric than that it seeks to replace. The choice of words for use in worship is one area where it is best to make changes slowly.

Structure and words are vital for worship and have long been so recognized. The importance of the various actions in worship is being increasingly appreciated. This is a significant change since Protestant worship especially has tended to be largely verbal, with actions discounted. To a large measure the new appreciation of action is due to a greater realization of the means of communication to the whole man. Man's participation in worship is not limited to the ears or mouth but involves his entire body. It is difficult for worship that is completely word-centered to demand as much of us or to express as fully the meaning of our worship as that involving the senses and the muscles.

Admirable as Quaker worship is, it is deficient in its use of the God-given parts of the body, except the ear and mouth.

We soon realize the limitations of words. If you doubt this, try translating an art form into words. It is difficult to capture in words the external appearance of a great building; it is impossible to do justice verbally to the experience of moving in and about a beautiful building. Language has its limits and must be supplemented as a means of communication. "Show me!" cries the heroine of *My Fair Lady* in her famous impatience with "Words!/ Words! Words!"

Actions are an important means of expressing meaning. Much of the great power of the sacraments comes from their ability to "show forth" the gospel rather than to tell forth the same material. This does not mean that words are any less important but that actions must be treated with more seriousness than in the recent past.

One of the lessons which revivalism should have taught us was that in order to move people spiritually you have to move them physically. The mourners' bench and saw-dust trail reflect a pretty good understanding of man's modes of expression, obsolete though these particular forms may be today. Instead, our middle-class inhibitions have nailed us down into tightly regimented rows of pews. It may well be that the introduction of church seating in parts of Europe during the fourteenth century was an unfortunate development. At any rate the "comfortable pew" has become a symbol of the lethargy of the modern church.

We would do well to reconsider our inhibitions which render us so immobile during worship. Actions come naturally to man. Children are taught not to dance and not to sing. Dancing and singing are natural means of expression to them, but as children mature they accept the inhibitions of civilization and stop dancing. One of the great advantages of jazz and country music is that they take seriously natural spontaneous forms of expression that we usually repress. Though we may not be willing to dance before the Lord as David did (II Samuel 6:14), the effort to "make merry before the Lord" (6:21) is as natural an impulse as the singing of a hymn of praise.

Part of the great power of actions is their ability to represent simultaneously several different levels of meaning. Thus what is done with bread and wine in the holy communion has its obvious nature as a ritual meal. But it also has the overtones of a redoing of the events of the Last Supper. At the same time it becomes a mime of the whole story of our salvation in God's taking our offering and giving ourselves back transformed. Unfortunately we have allowed the words to obscure the actions. St. Augustine called baptism a "visible word"[6] and the same applies to holy communion. If the actions were understood well enough, holy communion with far fewer words and more concentration on the dramatic showing forth of the events of redemption would be more expressive. The gestures of this sacrament need careful study as a form of communication.

One cannot deny the power of association in making actions meaningful. It would hardly be possible to invent new actions to convey meaning. The kiss of peace is a very ancient practice symbolizing reconciliation but it is totally unfamiliar to most Christians today. Reintroducing it, as has been tried in a number of cases, seems usually to produce the "giggle period." Probably new actions are

[6] *Tractates on the Gospel According to Saint John,* LXXX, 3.

as hard to come by as any other kind of symbol, and we are led to the same conclusions as with verbal symbols. Some old ones are moribund and ought to be forgotten, but new actions are difficult to secure simply by taking thought.

In recent years there has been more and more a concern in the churches to help the laity to understand that they are the ones who offer worship, not just the minister and the choir. The actions of worship belong to the layman just as much as to the clergy. Too often the layman has been passive and worship has become a spectator sport. Many actions belong to the layman: offering his praise through singing and reciting psalms, making his offering of money, and reciting prayer and the creed. There is no reason why a layman should not read the lessons. The offering of the bread and wine in holy communion ought to come from the laymen. One of the most expressive acts of worship is going forward to be given the bread and wine at holy communion. Words cannot express the significance of this act for those who are accustomed to it.

Even the various postures of worship are significant. At present there seems to be a growing preference for standing as the position for prayer, as if to express respect for the presence of God to whom it is offered. Kneeling is a subjective act which calls attention to one's humility and may be best for prayer of confession. Were the President of our country to enter a room we would stand out of respect for his presence, not draw attention to our humility by kneeling. It would be indeed ironical if Roman Catholics took all the kneelers out of churches at about the same time the Protestants all put them in! Sitting is justified for those times when God's Word is being expounded and we need to concentrate on its meaning. But for much of the time of worship we ought to be on our feet.

Motion, as revivalism knew full well, is a most satisfactory means of expressing worship. Processions have largely died out in Protestant worship, except in the marching of the choir. But processions by the congregation around the perimeter of the church, singing hymns on the way, can be a most expressive action. It may be that they would fare better if called Christian demonstrations. The racial demonstration in which marching is used to express one's beliefs may well be a secularized version of an ancient liturgical practice, the church procession to celebrate festivals.

In a world accustomed to seeing action on television, motion is recognized as an important form of expression. We are no longer in a radio era. More than word and noise is necessary if we are to express our worship to the best of our ability. We can no more afford to lounge in our pew while someone else does worship for us than we can be indifferent to the challenges of the world that scoffs at the "comfortable pew." The great value of actions is in giving the whole congregation a means of expressing their participation in worship.

Worship demands the use of forms. Some are adequate, others are not. All orders of worship, texts, and rubrics need to be appraised to make certain that the structures, words, and actions they provide are adequate means of expressing the substance of Christian worship. Ultimately the forms may be indifferent, but they are necessary vehicles for expressing the substance of worship. This may be a parallel to the incarnation, the divine becoming present beneath the veil of the human. One uses human forms to express the substance of his worship. Ultimately it is only the substance that matters, but being human we must use forms.

The positions we have taken here with regard to current forms of worship will seem most conservative to many people, especially to those who long to make worship "contemporary" and "relevant." But I am convinced that mere tinkering with the forms in an effort to update worship will not benefit us much. Until we have wrestled seriously with the question of what is the substance of worship, not just baptism or preaching but worship in general, not until we have done this do we have any right to talk about new forms. It profits little to contemporize we know not what. It may well be that if many Christians really found out what worship is they wouldn't want it. Especially were we to strip away the entertainment features provided for us, sweet music and even sweeter sermon stories, the substance of worship might appear quite different than we had imagined. Maybe we have too much worship today and too little understanding of it.

It is a renewal in understanding the substance of worship that must come first, not the invention of new forms. Otherwise we may simply be changing clothes on a manikin, wondering why it never comes alive no matter how avant-garde the garb may be.

A fresh understanding of the substance of worship may make us realize just how radical the ancient forms really are. We turn in the two following chapters to a more extensive look at the substance of worship. In Chapter VI we shall do a case study of the forms and substance used in baptism. In looking more closely at this one example of worship, we may be able to see the necessity of understanding the substance of worship before the forms can make much sense.

III
WORSHIP AND THE WORLD

The world as we know it is the world of time and space. It consists of the here and now of our own existence and the then and there of other lives. This is to say that all human life is historical life. Man lives out his years bounded by time and space. These are the conditions, the given, of human life. Likewise, each person is not only a creature in time but also of his time. We are conditioned by the time in which we live. The life we know is life in our own time, in our own fragment of existence. We cannot know life in any other way than as historical existence.

Christian worship takes history with the utmost seriousness. Indeed, this is the most obvious sense in which worship is worldly. A major portion of almost any service of Christian worship is given over to the reconsideration of historical events past and present. It is important to remember, of course, that historical existence is a matter of the present just as it is of the past. Christian worship involves the commemoration of events past, but it is not confined to them. Present life is an important part of the reconsideration of worship too.

The great strength of Christian worship is the seriousness with which it deals with past history. The outlines of Christian worship are based largely upon history, rather than upon speculation. Of course, myths are used to express such enduring truths as creation and judgment. The chief weakness of the forms used to express Christian worship is the frequent failure to accord present history the same attention given to past history. This is not a shortcoming inherent in the nature of Christian worship but of the forms we use. Christian worship at its best treats history, both past and present with equal seriousness. Neither time is to be neglected, since history is one and has its source in God.

For purposes of discussion, however, we will examine separately the relationship of worship and the world as manifested first in concern with past history and then the same concern with current history. Both are one but can be discussed more easily by being separated temporarily.

1

It does not take much reflection to see how many elements of Christian worship are a commemoration of past history. This is equally obvious in Jewish worship. Both religions take history seriously though some oriental religions regard it as vain and illusory. The most obvious elements of commemoration in Christian worship are those revolving around the reading of lessons from the Bible. Major portions of historical narrative are thus incorporated directly into most services of worship. Certainly not all the biblical material is historical; many sections include elements expressing a mythical understanding of the world and of God. But major portions proclaim "this happened." They are grounded in history and we recover it during each service of worship.

Commemoration is perhaps only slightly less obvious in the many hymns and psalms that recount the events of the history of salvation. Prayers and sermons also dwell frequently upon the recovery of past events. The sacraments too rehearse past history. In the eucharist the mime of the Last Supper is an obvious recalling of history. In early times the great prayer of the eucharist summarized the full biblical narrative of God's work. In a similar fashion, baptism is a recalling of events even in the act of baptizing in the present. The baptism of Jesus is rehearsed, but even more important is the showing forth of His death in which all men were potentially baptized.

The recovery of past events is a major part of Christian worship. Indeed, this seems so obvious that it is hardly necessary to document it further. We do need, however, to investigate what is commemorated, how this is done, and, most important of all, why it is done.

In worship we commemorate meaningful events. There is a parallel in our national holidays. We do not commemorate an abstraction of freedom; we celebrate the Fourth of July. Something happened on this day in 1776 that made freedom a possibility. Even Thanksgiving is based on an event. The Pilgrims held many thanksgivings but the harvest Thanksgiving of 1621 became the foundation still visible through all that has subsequently been built upon it. The commemoration of the event communicates the idea as well.

It is important to remember that the events commemorated in worship were of one piece with the rest of history as far as most people were concerned. They were secular events first of all and not religious events at all. And for most of the world they were forgotten as such. Only to the eyes of faith did these secular events have divine significance. W. H. Auden wrote:

> That even the dreadful martyrdom must run its course
> Anyhow in a corner, some untidy spot
> Where the dogs go on with their doggy life and the
>   torturer's horse
> Scratches its innocent behind on a tree.[1]

The events commemorated in worship passed on without any break in history as far as most people were concerned. The extraordinary thing about them is not that they were supernatural in form but so natural, the plain stuff of normal life.

The Exodus from Egypt became a central theme in Jewish worship, commemorated particularly in the celebration of the Passover. We must remember that except for the Hebrews, the Exodus was an economic and military event, not a religious one. It was a walk-out strike, and history is full of such occasions. Except to the Hebrews, it seemed such a mundane occurrence that the Egyptians failed to leave us any record of the Exodus.

The Hebrews, as soon as they found themselves safe, saw it otherwise. They discovered this same secular event to be an act of divine deliverance for them. Miriam's song reflects what the event became in their reconsideration: "Sing to the Lord, for he has triumphed gloriously" (Exodus 15:21). A piece of history had become a means by which one saw through to the ground of history. It remained history but for them it had been a moment of revelation, disclosing the nature of God.

[1]"Musée des Beaux Arts," *The Collected Poetry of W. H. Auden* (New York: Random House, 1945), p. 3.

A similar story could be told about the crucifixion. For most people it was an unimportant failure. Even the disciples walked away, having lost hope that "he was the one to redeem Israel" (Luke 24:21). If there had been newspapers it probably would have been buried on the back pages where notices of executions still occur. Barabbas might have been on page one. For most of the contemporaries the crucifixion was a purely secular event. Death comes to every man; the papers are full of obituaries.

Once again, small groups saw through the event to its meaning. Because of their faith in the resurrection, they found that in this defeat, God had nevertheless "triumphed gloriously." To faith it became an event that made all history have a new meaning. And yet it is the secular event, the execution of a condemned man, that is our Good Friday and plays so central a role in Christian worship.

The events commemorated in worship, then, are first of all secular events recognizable to any contemporary. The armies of Assyria, the military genius of Cyrus, a plague, all seem to be natural occurrences. But the eye of faith has selected them as means of seeing through to an ultimate significance. There is nothing spooky about these events; they are fragments of history. All demand the attention of the historian. Christianity indeed demands the services of the historian and insists that he be competent.

But just as no chemical analysis will ever prove that the bread and wine of the eucharist are anything but bread and wine (unless it be grape juice), so to the historian as historian the biblical events are ordinary history. It is only to the eye of faith that these events are transformed into events of divine disclosure. The non-believer saw what was happening, the believer witnessed what God was doing. The same rain falls on good and bad alike, the same event comes to two men, but to one it is mere chance, to another it is God's act.

The commemoration at the heart of Christian worship is secular history. Indeed it is the only kind of history there is. But the Christian sees God as acting within this history and so it also becomes the history of salvation. But it is history just the same, never less so. Paul Tillich says: "Wherever the divine is manifest, it is manifest in 'flesh,' that is, in a concrete, physical, and historical reality, as in the religious receptivity of the biblical writers."[2]

What matters about God's acts is that they are not disinterested. In traditional language, God acts to save man. His actions are for us. The biblical narrative sees His actions as not something unconnected and fragmentary. The communities of Israel and Christianity see behind these actions a plan of salvation. The events become comprehended within the framework of a covenant, or rather, a series of covenants. The God who acts, acts for His people. He acts supremely in the Christ event to reconcile the world to Himself (II Corinthians 5:19).

Each successive event in which the hand of God is seen is placed within the framework of the understanding of previous events. The God seen as giving the covenant at Mount Sinai is the God of the Exodus, and before that, the God of Abraham, Isaac, and Jacob. In this way each event has a permanent quality, for the understanding of

[2]*Biblical Religion and the Search for Ultimate Reality* (Chicago: University of Chicago Press, 1955), p. 5.

it colors the interpretation of succeeding events. Accordingly the record of each event is preserved, becoming frequently a part of worship where it influences the understanding of current events. The event that faith witnesses is preserved by the Jewish or Christian community and in turn helps preserve the community. It gives a center of meaning, it teaches us what it is to know ourselves as objects of God's love. And so both Judaism and Christianity are communities based upon their understanding of certain events as saving events in which God has acted for His people.

Our attention now turns to the manner in which this affects us in worship. Here we will be building upon some ideas set forth by Dom Odo Casel, O.S.B. (1886–1948), a German scholar whose work had tremendous influence on discussions of the theology of worship.[3] Casel is famous for his "mystery theology" that has been widely attacked and defended. One of the many fascinating aspects of his work is the way in which it opens possibilities for discussion between Catholics and Protestants.[4] Particularly interesting is the way in which this approach to worship in general bears parallels to the theology of preaching of such Protestant theologians as John Knox and H. H. Farmer.[5]

With regard to worship, the basic idea of Casel's mystery

[3]Of Casel's many writings, only one, *The Mystery of Christian Worship* (Westminster, Md.: Newman Press, 1962), has been published in English.

[4]For criticism of Casel, see E. Schillebeeckx, *Christ: The Sacrament of Encounter with God* (New York: Sheed and Ward, 1964), pp. 55–60. For a defense of the orthodoxy of Casel, see L. M. McMahon, "Towards a Theology of the Liturgy: Dom Odo Casel and the 'Mysterientheorie,'" *Studia Liturgica,* III (1964), pp. 129–54.

[5]John Knox, *The Integrity of Preaching* (New York: Abingdon, 1957), pp. 92–5 and H. H. Farmer, *Servant of the Word* (Philadelphia: Fortress, 1964), pp. 10–16.

theology is that in worship "it is the primaeval saving act which is made present."[6] That is as if to say, the historical saving event is made present to us in and through our acts of worship commemorating that event: "The church does what the Lord did, and thereby makes his act present. Christ himself is present and acts through the church, his *ecclesia,* while she acts with him. Both carry out the action."[7]

We must clarify this at several points. The historical event is unique and unrepeatable. Christianity does not have a cyclical view of history. If it did, the salvation event would be meaningless; Christ would have to die a million times. The event cannot be repeated; what is recovered is its saving power. But after all, this is all that makes the event significant. There was only one Exodus from Egypt, but the saving power of this event, the knowledge of God's gracious love for His people, is mediated through each celebration of the Passover. Calvary cannot be repeated, but the sacrificial love shown in this event can be proclaimed until the end of time.

Since the saving power of the original event is offered to us in our present, there is no advantage to those who were the contemporaries of it. The event becomes, in effect, our contemporary, for all that it signifies to us of God's love is recovered by us in the act of worship. The past event becomes our event insofar as it has power to save. In this sense Casel can speak of our living "our own sacred history."[8] All that matters in past history as far as our salvation is concerned is made present for us to appropriate. Kierkegaard reflected a similar concept:

[6]*Mystery of Christian Worship,* p. 124.

[7]Ibid. p. 141.

[8]Ibid. p. 124.

"For in relation to the absolute there is only one tense: the present. For him who is not contemporary with the absolute—for him it has no existence."[9]

That which is recovered in worship is the saving power of the event. The meaning of the event for one's being is transmitted in worship. But this is not simply a subjective matter of remembrance, it is based upon the objective re-presentation of actual events in worship. One does not simply understand what happened on Calvary as an intellectual abstraction; he experiences it as an event in which he is actively engaged by re-presenting it through worship. We relive Good Friday and thus experience the power of the original event through the re-enactment of it.

But how does the event become ours? Through re-presenting it we internalize the event. It becomes my event, a part of my situation in life, of my history. "This happened," becomes "this happened for me." And as a member of the community that shares this history, I find myself united to my fellow worshiper through sharing in things both worldly and holy. One can speak of worship as a means of God giving Himself anew. Whatever witness to His love for His creatures was manifested in past actions is again offered to me to appropriate in worship. Christ does not die anew when I worship and yet His sacrifice is re-presented to me in order for me to receive afresh His offering to me. Each service of worship becomes a new epiphany, a new showing forth of God's gracious action on my behalf. Very early in the history of the Church we note the development of forms for recalling the past actions of God for our present appropriation. Already present within Judaism was the orderly re-presen-

[9]Soren Kierkegaard, *Training in Christianity* (Princeton: Princeton University Press, 1957), p. 67.

tation of the events recorded in the Torah and in the prophets as these events were read each Sabbath in the synagogue. The Church soon developed its own orderly re-presentation of the new saving events that had determined its life. How much the New Testament is the byproduct of Christian worship may be debated but it is certain that it became a basic ingredient of such worship. Throughout its history the Church has utilized the Scriptures as a convenient means of recovering the events of salvation in worship. Many have experienced the peculiar power that the Scriptures often have when read in public worship, an experience quite different from that of reading the Bible in any other context.

The holy communion or eucharist (the great thanksgiving), to give it the most adequate name, is a constant means of recovering the climactic events of salvation history. It should be remembered, however, that what is celebrated in the eucharist comprehends the whole history of God's work and not simply those chronicled in the passion narrative. This might be more obvious if an Old Testament lesson and more psalmody were restored to the structure of the eucharistic rite.

Preaching, too, provides an orderly means of re-presenting the events of salvation. Indeed, the essence of preaching is in making present past events so that God may reveal Himself to us. When we hear the Word of God through preaching these events become our events. The gospel is made contemporary week after week in the act of preaching.

In recalling the events of salvation history one appropriates the action of God even though it is mediated in human form. None of the events that bear revelation are devoid of human participants and spectators. In recalling these events one is dependent upon the witnesses to the events. In the events of the ministry of Jesus one depends upon the witness of the earliest Church and then upon St. Paul, the evangelists, and other writers. Only certain events were preserved in the traditions of the early Church though the Fourth Gospel indicates there were many others in the ministry of Jesus (John 21:25). We depend on these written accounts. They make it possible for us to recall not only the individual events of Jesus' ministry but the mystery of God who gives Himself to man. Christianity is not just a religion about God but about God who takes the form of a servant to present Himself to man.

This is particularly true of the eucharist. St. Paul hands over to us that which he had received from the Lord, telling us to do this for the recalling (*anamnēsis*) of Him (I Corinthians 11:23–24). There has been much recent interest in the meaning of the word *anamnēsis*,[10] only feebly translated as "remembrance." Its import could better be covered by such terms as "recalling" or "re-presenting." That which happens in the eucharist, according to St. Paul, is that the meal becomes a means of making the Lord again present. It is not a memorial of Our Dead Leader as too often seems to be the case in the minds of many Protestants. It is the calling into action of Christ Himself as we ourselves obey the command "do this" (*touto poieite*) in celebrating the Lord's own Supper. *Anamnēsis*, then, is the bringing before our consciousness the actions of the Lord Himself. The Lord gives Himself to us with all His saving actions under the forms of this Supper.

The same theme is acted out in the course of the Chris-

[10]Gregory Dix, O.S.B., *The Shape of the Liturgy* (London: Dacre Press, 1945), p. 243–7.

tian year. The eucharist is not the only form of *anamnēsis.* The pattern of the Christian year is that of reliving the events of Christ's earthly ministry. We recapture these events in the re-enacting of what Christ has done. Our present post-Pentecostal life recalls the climactic events before Pentecost.

The Christian year, of course, involves a recapturing of events narrated in the Old Testament too. Though the Christian year is structured upon the ministry of Christ, this ministry is anticipated and indicated throughout the Old Testament. Throughout the course of the year, a large element of the Old Testament is used in the lessons, the psalms, and as a basis for much of preaching and hymnody. One can hardly participate in the events of the New Covenant without sharing in those of the Old Covenant. Father Charles Davis reminds us that Catholics need to understand the Old Testament in order to understand the mass.[11] This is true of all worship. The ministry of Christ is a continuation and climax of the work of God chronicled in the Old Testament. In worship one stands in on the events before the first century A.D. as well as those during it and since.

We must see the nature of worship as the recovering of these actions of God through our own acts of worship. Casel reminds us: "The congregation, by performing the rite, take part in the saving act, and thereby win salvation."[12] Worship is not a passive matter, not something sprayed in our faces by others. Worship is our doing. But in our doing God is also acting. There is a danger in overemphasizing our action, vital though that may be.

[11]Charles Davis, S. J., *Liturgy and Doctrine,* (London: Sheed & Ward, 1960), p. 37.

[12]*Mystery of Christian Worship,* p. 54.

What really matters, what keeps worship from being merely an idle performance is that in, with, and under our actions, God is acting. In Casel's words: "The essential thing is that some action of Christ's takes place. . . . It is not our feelings and our acts which count, but what God is doing."[13]

God as known in worship is acting to reconcile the world to Himself. It is unfortunate that we speak of the presence of God in worship. We would do better to speak of the action of God. God is acting in giving Himself to us in our worship. God makes Himself known in worship as a judging and forgiving, a loving and providing God, not as an abstract presence. We encounter Him by entering into a gracious personal relationship, not as a static matter.[14] What we encounter of God in our worship is His action made known through past acts, and given to us anew in the re-enactment of these events. God is not merely present in worship; He is active in it. He gives Himself to us in worship, thus enabling us to give ourselves to others.

Our worship occurs in history as we know it in everyday life. Yet it bridges history in re-presenting to us the context of events past and thereby changing the inner history of our lives. The outer history, that which is observable in the day by day living of our lives, may not change much. But the inner history, our stance on life, our basic mental attitude, can be greatly affected by what happens in worship.

In worship one does not become any less a historical

[13]Ibid. p. 157.

[14]Cf. Donald Baillie, *Theology of the Sacraments* (New York: Scribners, 1957), p. 49. Schillebeeckx's statement that religion is "essentially a personal relation of man to God" seems to concur (*Christ: The Sacrament of the Encounter with God*, p. 4).

self. Indeed he becomes more such. Because of its trans-historical quality, worship gives us a wider experience of history by making us share in the meaning-events, the clues to history, the moments of revelation. I remain bound by the years of my birth and death, but the years between these personal events derive meaning because of the events beyond them given to me in worship.

The events of salvation are no longer merely past tense. The tense of worship is a present time that includes both past and future. The reality of past events becomes mine as I participate in public worship. These events have a reality prior to me and independent of my own existence. They happened whether I care or not.

Through the acts of worship the saving efficacy of these past events is again offered to me. They span history to give meaning to present life. This is what we mean by the trans-historical character of Christian worship. The redemptive power of these events is made mine in worship. What Christ did for me on Calvary, I can appropriate in worship. The deliverance from Egypt becomes my own personal event as I experience for myself the gracious love of God in worship. These past events become my history, part of my being. In this sense, worship tremendously expands our participation in history.

Stated in this fashion, the problem of worship becomes a time mystery. The central concern is the trans-historical quality that mediates past events to our present lives. Unfortunately, theologians of the Middle Ages treated worship as a space mystery, particularly with regard to the eucharist but also, to a certain degree, in the matter of the other sacraments. Even the Reformers, while rebelling against the medieval answers to worship, could not avoid stating the problems in spatial terms. Luther found Christ ubiquitous, and Calvin worried about getting us up to heaven where Christ was enthroned. Was not this a wrong statement of the whole question? Is not the real problem primarily a time mystery and only secondarily a spatial one?

It would seem so if we were to think consistently of worship as action in which God acts. Surely His real action is a more biblical concept than His real presence. The biblical accounts tell us what God does, not what He is. The same ought to apply in worship as well. We recognize what God is doing in making us contemporaries of His actions. We know Him as acting in our actions of worship. We might do better to avoid using the language of space and substance until we have explored more fully the language of time and history.

In worship, past history plays an extremely important role, for the events by which God has acted in the past are delivered to me and made my events. No longer is past history an alien affair; it becomes a part of my understanding of myself and the world. The saving power of past events is given to me and becomes a part of my ability to live as a Christian in the present.

II

Christian worship, however, is based on present events as well as on past history. It is concerned with what God is doing as well as with what He has done. Unfortunately the forms of Christian worship often neglect this. God's present activity seems too often to be like the dark side of the moon, acknowledged to be there but never glimpsed in our worship. No one denies that God is working in the world today unless it be to maintain that God is dead. If one believes that God is alive, one also believes that He acts. Deism is dead and no one cares to revive the watchmaker concept of God. If God had been a celestial watchmaker who went off and left the world ticking, it would be hard to know why one should worship Him. But most Christians would affirm that they conceive of God as acting in the world today even though the forms of our worship do little to express this.

There is good reason for this reticence, of course. The danger of pointing out the footprints of God is a real one. What if some new monster has landed upon our island and we be following his trail to our destruction? One hesitates to be very explicit about what God is doing. It can too easily lead to superstition. There are other dangers. God may be acting in judgment of us or our way of life and at the same time be acting for us as does a parent in punishing a child through love. This is a bit hard to explain to children. They never seem to appreciate being spanked because they are loved. We find it hard to detect the hand of God in events that thwart our ambitions or change our way of life. One must be wary of anyone who says, "Lo, the hand of God." After all, "God moves in a mysterious way" and we can hardly be expected always to recognize a "frowning providence."

There do seem, however, to be some ways in which our worship can reflect God as acting in our time. First of all, the orders of creation and of society that make civilized life possible depend upon His will. These orders impinge upon our lives constantly and we can reflect the orders in our worship. We can also trust that God is acting in our times in ways which are not obvious to us. We can live in the faith that whatever God is doing is worthy of our trust. This is the courage to deny that

> . . . we are here as on a darkling plain
> Swept with confused alarms of struggle and flight,
> Where ignorant armies clash by night.[15]

We can live in the faith that life, the totality of all life, makes sense because ultimately all being depends upon God alone. Both the orders of life and our personal life of trust in God's activity help us understand present history as being just as significant as God's saving acts in the past.

Our problem then is in taking seriously God as working in the world today without falling into the danger of undue particularity. Actually this may not be as difficult as it might sound. We have already seen that the Bible depicts God as acting in events that we would call secular events: the escape of slaves, sickness in the army, and famine in Palestine. Yahweh, the God of Israel, was not a very "religious" god. In the Old Testament, more often than not, revelatory events occur along some dusty road rather than in the temple. The question that greets Elijah in solitude is typical: "What are you doing *here*, Elijah?" (I Kings 19:9 & 13). God is where the action is and his prophet is expected to be on the spot too. We are not called upon to look for events with the label "religious" upon them to understand God working in our time.

In the 1964–65 New York World's Fair, God was represented by a number of official exhibits. There was a Vatican pavilion, a Protestant one, another for the Orthodox—to say nothing of Billy Graham, the Christian Scientists, and Mormons. Each of these exhibits tried to show what the Church (or rather an individual portion of it) is doing today by presenting scenes of the Church in mission in

[15]Matthew Arnold, "Dover Beach."

numerous activities. But I would guess that what God is doing was shown more directly (and sometimes more artistically) by some of the mammoth scientific exhibits, with their emphasis on the new possibilities of freedom made possible by technology, or in the pavilions of the nations where the conditions of life are being radically changed. Changes in living conditions are not all necessarily good, but if God be working at all in the world it would seem that He works where it matters, in changing the possibilities for the existence of His creatures. The reflection of God's acting certainly was not confined to the exhibits of the churches at the Fair.

This is not to say, by any means, that God does not act in and through His Church. But the Church always seems in danger of hugging itself to death for having God whereas it is only the center of the circle of His love. The challenge to the Church is to try to understand what God is doing in the world and to join Him in His work. In a sense this is what the churches did in nineteenth-century America in pioneering our American system of higher education. Certainly the church colleges of the nineteenth century, in helping to bring higher education to a vast number of people, set up one of the prerequisites of modern life. Of 182 permanent colleges and universities founded before the Civil War, all but 27 were denominational in origin.[16] Perhaps it is time now for the Church to turn the college loose in order to begin exploring new forms for urban living. Parallel stories might be told with regard to the development of elementary education, medical facilities, child care, and other institutions that have

[16]Donald G. Tewksbury, *The Founding of American Colleges and Universities Before the Civil War* (New York: Teachers College, Columbia University, 1932), p. 90.

become absolutely necessary for the existence of modern society. In our present perplexities as to how the Church can exercise its servanthood in ministering to men, it is helpful to realize that sometimes we have been enabled to do miraculously well.

God is acting both in the world and in the Church, and worship needs to reflect this fact of being. All too often worship seems to indicate that God has been relatively inactive, or at least quiet, since II Peter was finished about A.D. 135 thus completing the canonical books of the New Testament. If this were the case, then God would be dead.

Roman Catholicism has done fairly well in preserving in its worship the semblance of the continuity of God's actions through the cult of the saints. What matters in the saints, of course, is not what they did but what God did through them. In some of the mass prayers on saints' days, for instance, there are expressions of God's guidance in the lives of the saints. A prayer on the day of St. Lawrence, Martyr says: "Give us the grace, Lord, to extinguish the fires of our evil passions, as you gave St. Lawrence the strength to triumph over the flames of his cruel torture."[17] Another, on the feast of Sts. Simon and Jude, Apostles, reads: "Through your apostles, St. Simon and St. Jude, you have allowed us, Lord, to learn about yourself."[18] The saints act, but we worship God and praise Him for what He does through them. Of course the commemoration of the saints stops short of the present. With extreme caution one hardly dares tread past the threshold of our own century, and one tends to overlook what God is doing with the saints and non-saints of our time. But it may well be

[17] *Our Parish Prays and Sings* (Collegeville, Minn.: Liturgical Press, n.d.), p. 193.
[18] Ibid. p. 207.

that Protestants should understand the saints as witnesses to the continuity of God's actions. At least it would remind us that the Almighty did not punch out on a celestial time clock when the New Testament was completed.

Of course, the cult of the saints is a very limited way of using a symbolic few to show the continuity of God's work. Undoubtedly the Christ event is a high point, giving meaning to the whole work of God. But it sweeps on to Christ's statement that it is necessary for Him to leave that the Holy Spirit may come. Our temptation is to live on the other side of Pentecost, whereas we are given post-Pentecostal time in which to witness God's work.

By no means is God's work confined to that of the Church—as our worship too often suggests in praying "for the peace of Jerusalem" (Psalm 122:6):

> "May they prosper who love you!
> Peace be within your walls,
> and security within your towers!"

There is nothing wrong with this as long as one does not stop there. But we are also called upon to pray for the peace of Nineveh and Babylon—the world. And that is not quite so easily done, especially when the Ninevites turn out to be Communists and the Babylonians are Black Muslims.

It is all too easy for the worshiping Church to forget other subjects of God's love, namely all men, the Church outside of the Church. It is all too easy to pass by on the other side and to thank God (which is an act of worship) that we are not like other men. But God acts for other men as He does for us. We have no monopoly on His love. The Church outside of the Church is other men.

Christ died for them just as surely as for those within the Church. God is working through them as constantly as with those who are Church members, the Church inside of the Church. Our worship has been prone to forget that the only peace of Jerusalem is the peace of the whole world.

Perhaps St. Augustine should be criticized for speaking of two cities "formed by two loves: the earthly by a love of self, . . . the heavenly by the love of God."[19] One may differentiate between the loves of man. But should not one begin rather with the love of God? Isn't this closer to things as they really are? We can hardly say that God's love is divided unless we believe in a limited atonement. Calvary was not just for those with tickets. God's love comes to men in different ways, but the gift of life—to stand up and walk about in the sun for awhile—is hardly limited to the Christian. There is one divine love given to all men, though in different ways. Surely this is a part of our worship.

The Church inside the Church has a special role to play in this love. It is that of servant, God's hired man, God's help. The glory of the Church inside of the Church is that it is called upon to serve the Church outside of the Church. God's love is given to those inside of the Church, enabling them to serve. They know their Master's voice and are called to obedient service in His world. We have spoken of the Church as God's pioneer, but it also has the less dramatic task of cultivating land where other ploughs have broken the sod. The Church serves in the slow misery of the dying of ways of life, as well as in bathing the newborn.

We have spoken of the reality of God acting in the

[19] *City of God*, XIV, 28.

world and our need to take this seriously. But in order to reflect this in our worship we need to have means of understanding more explicitly the nature of God's working. We need to know more than the fact that God acts in the world and yet avoid the danger of knowing too much about how He works. We need to look particularly at the history of our times in two ways: what is going on in the world about us, and what is going on in the world about us as it directly impinges on our individual selves.

In trying to understand the "signs of the times," a habitual Christian sport, our best approach is that of seeing God as source of all that makes life possible. For convenience we shall make a distinction between the orders of creation, the various ways in which men's lives are subject to the physical universe, and the orders of social structure, the ways in which men live together. Both are part of God's continual creating and redeeming activity. Indeed it is difficult to distinguish between creation and redemption; Chapter 1 of St. Matthew's Gospel makes little sense without Genesis 1.

We can no longer think of the orders of nature or of social life as unchanging. Progress in medical research has given us a significantly new relationship to the physical universe. New forms of urban living have significantly modified the possibilities of social life.

The value of speaking of the orders, though, is indicated by the word "ordered" itself, from the same root as "ordained." It is not to say "Whatever is, is right," but that "whatever is" ultimately has its being through God. The basic orders of nature, the constant rhythms of life, can be seen as reflections of God's continual creating activity. This is even more the case as the given conditions of life change from age to age. The possibility of living elsewhere than on earth is perhaps the most dramatic present expectation of change in the possibilities for us of the created orders. There are many others, perhaps less spectacular, but of great importance. While making rubbings of early New England tombstones, I became aware of how frequently mother and newly-born infant were buried together. This is not a condition of life in America today. Pregnancy is not the threat to life it once was. Only one birth in 3125 is fatal to the mother today. Our relation to nature has changed radically in this single instance as in many others. The elimination of distance as a barrier to human communication is another change in man's relation to the orders of creation, giving us freedom unthought of in previous generations.

The Bible speaks in the creation story of the world as being created so that God "saw everything that he had made, and behold, it was very good" (Genesis 1:31). Our possibilities for relating to this same universe are changing. The world as presented to us still reflects the continuing creating work of God. No doubt it was very good, and is now very good, and shall be very good, but all in different ways. We are confronted with changes in the way the created order is encountered by man, and we should recognize in this the continuity of creation.

The social structures of life, too, reflect both permanency and change. Social units of family, community, and state endure, but they are never the same. My fatherhood is not what fatherhood was for my father and certainly not what it was for my grandfather. It is hard to tell whether changes in the nature of the city or the nation are more obvious. And yet the basic natures of family, community, and state have strong elements of permanency. The family remains a small nucleus of love and nurture based upon physical relationship. City and nation remain mutual associations for common tranquility and for enhancing life.

One must acknowledge the presence of sin in all the social structures. In a poem entitled "September 1, 1939," the date of the beginning of World War II, W. H. Auden reflects:

> Into this neutral air
> Where blind skyscrapers use
> Their full height to proclaim
> The strength of Collective Man,
> Each language pours its vain
> Competitive excuse:
> But who can live for long
> In an euphoric dream;
> Out of the mirror they stare,
> Imperialism's face
> And the international wrong.[20]

We would hesitate to call all the changes of social structures divinely inspired. Man is given the terrible risk of freedom to make what he will of these structures. And yet even in the use of this freedom one can see the gift of God. And one can trust that He is working in, with, and under these same sin-ridden structures to bring new possibilities of being to us.

The very ambiguity of the social structures is big with the promise of new freedom. In the emergence of new nations, in the emergence within our country of those victimized by lack of opportunity, and in the new mobility of man, one can see new freedom developing, new dimensions added to life. One does not want to say, "Lo here,

[20]*Collected Poetry*, p. 58.

lo there" for each new development, but one is excited to believe that changes in our social environment reflect the continuous creating activity of God no less than do those in our relation to the physical universe. The Church's problem is not modern man, but man who refuses to be fully modern, remaining unfree, retarded, immature.

Once again we are forced back to a doctrine of being. To see God as acting in the world is possible first because Christians understand the world as ultimately dependent upon Him and, secondly, since they consider His work of creation a constant one. In speaking of God's activity in creating new possibilities for life, one can discuss His action as the key to the present history of the world.

It is time now to internalize this discussion and to reflect upon how what God is doing in the world is reflected in the life of the individual. How does what God is doing in the world affect my own unique self? There are several ways of analyzing this. The one we shall use is that of antiquity, though the ancient expressions of it are no longer sufficient. It is to speak of divine providence.

There was a time when trust in divine providence was much more explicit than we would care to make it today. The dark side of it is a form of determinism, a lack of freedom. Edward Johnson, the Puritan historian, believed: "The Lord was pleased to command the wind and seas to give us a jog on the elbow, by sinking the very chief of our shipping in the deep and splitting them in shivers against the shores."[21] The Puritan could see the fingerprints of God smeared on each and every event. Life in the Bay Colony was a succession of thanksgivings

[21] *Wonder-Working Providence,* edited by J. Franklin Jameson (New York: Scribners, 1910), p. 253.

and fasts as men responded to divine bounty or disfavor. None of us would care to be so explicit in fathoming the workings of providence.

Yet it is a pity that providence has been pushed into the background of theological discussion because of distortions. The essential concept is that of a divine *pronoia* (foresight, providence). One lives in the trust that God provides for us individually in a way that is beyond our comprehension. The divine *pronoia* consists of the ultimate wisdom that guides our destinies. It is the opposite of the cruel belief in meaningless fate. *Pronoia* is an affirmation that God is with us.

For our own life the significance of *pronoia* is the trust that it elicits. Paul's challenge sums it up neatly: "If God is for us, who is against us?" (Romans 8:31). It is trust, not in any contingent matter, not in trust itself, but in God. Without this trust the world is a collection of meaningless flashes. The trust that nothing can remove us from the love of God is the foundation of Christian faith. It does not mean that each detail in life conceals a divine message like the symbolism in some novel. But it is the enabling power to live with a confidence otherwise impossible.

Paul Tillich speaks of it as the "courage to be." Despite all temptation to the contrary, he finds that trust in the ground of our being gives us the possibility of facing the world courageously.[22] The ancient doctrine of providence has the same quality. It gives man the possibility of a new attitude to life. One dares to have the boldness to trust that no matter what happens God wills the good of His creatures and is working to bring it about. This has radical consequences for one's style of living and ought to be reflected in worship.

22Paul Tillich, *The Courage To Be* (London: Fontana, 1962), Ch. 6.

One of the most immediate consequences of this possibility is reflected in baptism, particularly infant baptism. The person who has been baptized has, in a passive fashion, received a pledge to him of the divine *pronoia.* One can understand how Luther could call baptism "a matter so great, gracious, and full of comfort."[23] Baptism is a visible sign of providence. It shows forth the prior love of God that claims man and the love that is given to him throughout life.

The doctrine of providence is a personal realization that the God who is working in the orders of creation and the structures of society is also a God who provides for His individual children. To live in trust is to know that the world, despite its ugliness and sin, is the area in which God's love is at work for me. It is to live with bold confidence that ultimately nothing can "separate us from the love of God in Christ Jesus our Lord" (Romans 8:39).

We have laid out two ways in which one knows God as working in present history: in the structures of creation and society and in one's trust in divine providence. The question that must now concern us is how these elements of history are reflected in our worship or, more specifically, how they *can be* reflected in it. This cannot be easily answered. If it could, we would not be faced with the problem confronting us in the neglect of this area.

One way to approach this question is by returning to our definition of worship as standing outside of one's normal consciousness for reconsideration and response. We will proceed on this basis. In worship we reconsider what we know already. We know that the Lord is at work in the world around us, and yet we don't know it con-

[23]"The Holy and Blessed Sacrament of Baptism," *Luther's Works* (Philadelphia: Muhlenberg Press, 1960), XXXV, 42.

stantly. In worship we recollect the true nature of being. This means we rediscover that God is working through the orders of creation and society. This we knew all along, but it rarely comes to our consciousness outside of worship. Worship becomes a time of reconsidering the world *sub specie aeternitatis.* In this sense it becomes a means of encountering the world on a deeper level than that of our normal consciousness.

Worship also becomes a time of reflection on what God is doing with and for us. The nature of our being as subject to divine *pronoia* becomes clearer in worship. There is a deeply personal level to worship that should not be obscured by talk of corporateness. We rediscover the nature of our own individual being in worship, as well as that of the world.

Worship should also be response to what one has discovered about God's present activity in the world. To a considerable measure, most of the contemporary reference in worship takes the form of gratitude expressed by means of praise for what God is doing. This takes place in the singing of hymns, in various prayers of praise, in the psalter, and in other ways. The offering of the bread and wine in the eucharist is a symbolic act of returning our present world to God to be used by Him in making His action known to us.

By these various acts we reflect our gratitude for what God is doing. Christian praise is based upon the activity of God, both past and present. It reflects our response to what God is doing in the orders and in our own self-understanding. Confession is a showing forth of our responsibility for the ways in which we have collectively and individually gone against what we understand God to be doing. It testifies both to our life in sin and to our trust in a God who acts to forgive. In more ways than we may expect, we respond in our worship to what we understand God to be doing in the here and now. Even so, this response to present action is not nearly as obvious as our response in worship to His actions in past history.

How can the reconsideration and response to God's present activity be made more conspicuous in worship? It is easy to say the ways by which it cannot. Holy Scripture is limited by a canon that has remained constant for well over a millennium. Yet the eye of faith that the biblical writers reflect so constantly is desperately needed to reflect contemporaneous divine actions. We would be nearer if we could understand, as the biblical writers did, that secular events are the only kind there are and thus are precisely the kind God uses to reveal Himself. The faith that can seek to understand events in God is not a monopoly of the biblical writers and editors. It is needed to worship God in our world in our time and space.

Structurally the elements best able to bear this understanding can be sorted out. It would seem that some of the characteristics of the worship of the central churches in American Protestantism offer great possibilities here, even though they have not always been fulfilled. This is particularly true of preaching and free prayer.

The great characteristic of preaching is that it is contemporary. Even when exegeting an ancient text, preaching is (or should be) expressed in the language of our time. The gospel is made our contemporary through preaching. The power of preaching to make past events present often results in a deeper understanding of what is happening today. This is not simply the result of any crude application. The power of the spoken word to illumine our own times is not by any means confined to preaching, but this is the aim of all preaching. In preaching, God as He has acted in times past is held up so we can see how He continues to act. Thus each sermon is a disclosure of the divine activity, at least if it deserves to be called a sermon. And this is the terrible risk that we must take.

Probably all that can possibly be said on the relative merits of free prayers and set forms was said in the seventeenth and eighteenth centuries. Strong arguments were advanced by partisans for both practices. Quite possibly each was right, though this possibility did not seem to enter the minds of the disputants. The great value of set forms in reflecting the present world is in expressing the natures of the orders of life insofar as they are constants. Some prayers regarding the nature of the physical universe (as thankfulness for the bounty of nature or petitions for averting catastrophes), or the orders of society (for the preservation of the king, i.e. nation), have permanent usefulness inasmuch as these aspects of the orders are relatively stable. But the great advantage of free prayer at its best is that it can seek to express the ways in which God is changing man's relation to his universe and changing the structures of society. Set prayers reflect the changeless aspects of the orders; free prayers seek to interpret the way in which they are changing. In either case, prayer reflects God as acting both through the changeless and the changing orders that make civilized life possible.

Essentially, then, making worship reflect God's present action is the problem of being true to the nature of God. If God be a God who acts in the here and now, then the need is for worship to be more fully worldly, since this is the nature of God. The enemy of the Church is not secularity but idolatry, the worship of the wrong god. And yet this is precisely the problem we face. We are too prone to worship a God who is dead, at least as far as being involved in the world is concerned. Worship that takes seriously divine action in past history—but ignores the same activity in the present—comes close to idolatry, since it does not truly reflect the nature of God. Perhaps the best testimony that God is dead occurs in the worship of Him in the past tense only.

It is when God is worshiped in accordance with His nature that worship becomes truly worldly. This comes when we take seriously the worldliness of God, that all that is depends upon His constant creating and redeeming activity. Here then the world is granted the full seriousness and the only seriousness that it deserves as the arena of God's action. Christian worship refuses to allow us to escape the world. At its very heart is history, both past and present. We discover God in what He does both in other times and in our own, and to this we respond in worship.

IV

THE WORLDLINESS OF WORSHIP

Our understanding of worship is greatly hampered by a false mystique. We tend to approach worship as if it involved the cultivation of an otherworldly atmosphere. All too often this involves a faint touch of quaintness. We try to make worship somehow different from the rest of life, and the easiest way to do this seems to be by a retreat from all those things most familiar to us. We want to make a gulf between what we do in worship and what we do in the rest of life. It is all too easy to do so.

This false mystique of worship is apparent in many of the words and art forms that most people have come to associate with religion. Most of us wouldn't be caught dead anywhere else singing the sentimental hymn music we use so often in Church. The greatest danger of the peculiar language that we use in worship is that it becomes not a means of approaching the otherness of God, but simply an escape mechanism from the world as we know it. The same is true of the atmosphere that many have come to associate with worship, "casting a dim religious light," stained-glass attitudes, and the thunder of organ pedal stops. The peril in all these is that they tend to make worship a means of deliberate escape from the world. The retreat to the past, the relish for what is quaint, the cult of the esoteric, all these are signs of a false mystique that misunderstands the very nature of Christian worship by seeking to ignore its worldliness.

Perhaps the best proof of this attitude is the grim seriousness with which we are accustomed to approach worship. Watch a choir as they are robing before worship. They laugh and talk and are themselves. But once the procession begins they become different persons afraid to be caught smiling. The rest of us, too, approach worship with a seriousness unlike that of any other occasion.

How have we forgotten that worship is joyful? Other religions seem to have preserved this understanding better than Christians have. Most of us would be shocked at the idea of making "merry before the Lord." It does not fit our stained-glass mystique about worship. Yet other religions have shown us that dancing can be a very legitimate part of worship. I do not speak of those intellectual experiments, tried in some churches, of having professional dancers perform in worship. This only increases the false seriousness of worship. I speak of dance as a means of worship for the whole congregation. In nineteenth-century America the Shakers used dancing as a part of their worship and we could learn something from them.

Even our singing tends to be on the lugubrious side. For every "Hallelujah Chorus" there seems to be a dozen hymns shrouded in a minor key. Perhaps we ought to heed the Psalmist:

> Make a joyful noise to the
> Lord, all the lands!
> Serve the Lord with gladness!
> Psalm 100:1–2

Life is hardly as joyless as we seem to picture it in our

worship. Some contemporary foot-tapping music might be a great help in being more true to our daily world.

We could learn from children who often seem to get so much pleasure out of singing praises and praying. Romano Guardini has a famous chapter on "The Playfulness of the Liturgy." The liturgy, he says, "unites art and reality in a supernatural childhood before God."[1]

At the heart of the false mystique about worship is a mistaken notion of things spiritual. We have forgotten that God is a worldly God and that the way to worship Him is not by escaping this world but by approaching it in the dimension of depth. The God whom we worship, after all, is the God whom we know as Creator. The creation stories in Genesis make it dramatically obvious that all that is depends upon God for its being. Other religions often tended to make the world seem like a major mistake, something that happened when gods had a bad day. But Genesis not only insists that God created the world but that He created it "good." "And God saw everything that he had made, and behold, it was very good" (Genesis 1:31). This is a repeated theme in the first creation narrative. All that is depends upon God and is created good. Creation constantly becomes beclouded and besmirched with sin, but God continues His creating action in relating Himself to the world.

One does not meet God by escaping from time and space. A Buddhist may try to free himself from these to obtain *nirvana*. But this is not the Christian way. A Christian meets God within this world by coming to a deeper understanding of the nature of the world itself and what God is doing in it. There is, to be sure, a subtle tradition within Christianity, inherited from platonism and break-

[1] *The Church and the Catholic and the Spirit of the Liturgy* (New York: Sheed and Ward, 1935), p. 181.

ing out from time to time in various forms of mysticism that try to escape from the giveness of life, to reach an area where time and space are transcended. The more natural way to worship the creator God would be to meet Him on His terms, that is, to seek to encounter Him within His world. We need not try to be more spiritual than God. We must not turn our backs on what God has done and is doing in order to know Him. To be truly spiritual is to be truly worldly. This does not mean worldly in a crass sense, but in the sense of perceiving the true nature of being and responding to it appropriately. Dietrich Bonhoeffer wrote: "I never experience the reality of God without the reality of the world or the reality of the world without the reality of God."[2] To treat "spiritual" and "worldly" as opposites is to try to out-spiritualize God.

One might make a distinction between the genuinely spiritual, seeking the knowledge of God, and the falsely spiritual, the spiritualistic, the seeking of the otherworldly. Christianity is spiritual but not spiritualistic. It has nothing to do with various spiritualisms that deny the reality of finite existence. "The Word," after all, "became flesh and dwelt among us, full of grace and truth" (John 1:14). Since New Testament times, Christianity has battled docetists, gnostics, Christian Scientists, and others who wanted to make it spiritualistic. The Christian way to being truly spiritual is by being deeply worldly.

I

If we look at the forms and materials of Christian worship we see how directly and unashamedly worldly they are. In

[2]*Ethics*, edited by Eberhard Bethge (New York: Macmillan, 1965), p. 195.

the first place, Christian worship is consciously and deliberately performed within history. Worship is done in the here and now. Each Sunday is an unique time: the first after Easter, 1966, or some other specific date. We Westerners are even inclined to watch the minutes in worship: 11:00 a.m. to noon is the time in our day for worship. The place too, is designated: St. Vitus-in-the-Vale Community Church, corner of Broad and High Streets, or some such specific location. Our worship is part of our time-kept week and located in our well-mapped space. It is obviously located in time and space.

When we look at what is used in worship we find how much the time and space categories of the world determine our spiritual worship. This paradox is hinted at by St. Paul when he speaks of presenting "your bodies as a living sacrifice, holy and acceptable to God, which is your spiritual (*logikos*) worship" (Romans 12:1). Worship does not seek to avoid the tangibility of the physical world. Physical substances serve a vital role in worship.

At the heart of baptism is the use of water. Holy Communion revolves around the use of bread and wine. And lest we think that non-sacramental worship is any less physical, we should remember that the spoken word consists of sound waves and that sound waves are every bit as physical (though invisible) as any other substance. Things are at the center of our worship and worship revolves around their several uses. This "thingness" of worship is often overlooked in attempts to "spiritualize" it, yet printed texts, sound waves, and bread and wine are all necessary tools used in doing our worship.

Furthermore, the things used in our worship are remarkably ordinary. They come from the center of our physical and social lives: food, drink, and talk. One looks in vain for any esoteric substances. Even the precious wedding ring is available at any jewelry store. And it is the exception; the substances used in the rest of worship are as inexpensive as they are common.

Turn on any faucet and water flows forth. Here is a substance that covers two-thirds of the earth's surface. Could anything be more common? The same water that washes us in baptism is the water that bathes us each day. The same liquid that is used in the laver of regeneration drives our generators, bubbles from drinking fountains, nourishes our lawns, and washes our dishes. One could hardly imagine a substance less esoteric.

In the eucharist we do not feast on the nectar and ambrosia of Olympian gods. Quite to the contrary, here are the staples of life, ordinary food and drink. Anyone who has been on second-class trains in Italy knows how common bread and wine are. Everyone comes on board with a loaf of bread and a bottle of wine. In our society it is easy to forget how basic bread and wine are to the diets of many nations. They are life itself. Take away bread and wine and you deprive many nations of their staples.

Nor is there anything special about the bread and wine. Look at the bread. It comes from wheat grown at a profit, flour milled at a profit, and bread baked at a profit. Perhaps somewhere along the way it has been stored in government bins, sold by the ton by a broker, carried by the railroads, and delivered by members of the teamsters' union. In short, it is an image of our whole social and economic structure. It would be hard to imagine anything more worldly than bread. The same applies to wine. Grapes picked by migrant workers, pressed and bottled mechanically, the whole process of distribution leads inevitably to the retailer and consumer. And so do countless other products. We have here the world's work, sweat, and cash. We offer and receive the products of the world at God's altar. Politics, economics, and sociology are all summed up in the communion elements, to be taken, blessed, broken, and given back to us as gifts from God.

Look too at what we do in worship. How ordinary our actions are! The spoken word is the most common form of human communication. One has only to reflect upon the thousands of words we utter each day to realize how completely dependent we are upon the spoken word. We relate to those about us chiefly by means of speech. And the same means becomes the key form in expressing Christian worship.

The most common social act of families, friends, and business associates is that of a meal together. It may be a hurried moment to "grab a bite" together or a formal dinner. Eating together provides a constant form of social intercourse. The central rite of Christendom, the eucharist, is basically a common meal. To be sure, it is a formalized type of meal. But it once was a full meal, quite different from our modern satisfaction with a minute sip of wine and a taste of bread. At any rate, the bread ought to be real bread, bought from the local bakery and not some tasteless substitute. The eucharist is a meal that we eat and drink together, not some esoteric act.

Nor should we forget that our worship is performed by humans. We meet our neighbors, not angels, in church. "Come, see a man," said the woman at the well, and Christ continues to speak to us through the words of men. The sacraments, too, demand a person to minister to others.

It is hardly necessary to point out how common such acts as singing, walking, standing, listening, and washing are. We do them every day in church and out of church. Once again one is struck by the ordinariness of our acts of worship. It would be hard to find any actions more common than the ones we use in worship. Worship uses the world instead of escaping from it.

The things we use and what we do in worship certainly do not suggest withdrawal from the world. Quite to the contrary, worship thrusts us out into a wider encounter with the world. This is in contrast to some of our sentimental hymns, more often than not heretical: "Sweet hour of prayer! That *calls me from a world of care*," or "I come to the garden *alone*." This is part of the mystique of otherworldliness. But worship isn't otherworldly. Worship brings a larger slice of life into our consciousness.

We use the things of the world in our worship in order to understand the true nature of all that is. Bread becomes not just bread but a means of discovering Christ in, with, and under the things of this life. Water becomes a pledge to us of the steadfast love of our God. And ordinary sound waves become the way in which the Word of God is proclaimed to men.

The importance of the use of things and actions in worship is that they enable us to encounter all things and all actions on a deeper level. One reviews the nature of all being as derived from God. This may be nothing new to us except in that we constantly forget what we know full well. Worship becomes a continual rehearsal, always prompting our memory, as we act out the nature of our being.

In all this we learn anew the worldliness of God. Worship is worldly because God is. We discover anew the dependence of all that is upon His will and action. Two theological doctrines come to our mind particularly: the doctrine of creation and that of providence. God works creating the world, not only as past action but constantly affecting the ways in which man responds to his natural environment, as well as the structure of society. At the same time, one can trust that God works in a way to give meaning to his own life. We review the ways in which the Church understands God to have acted in times past. History, we realize, is the realm in which God has acted and is acting now. In all this, worship is making us more fully conscious of what is going on in the world, not by superficially scanning the latest headlines, but by giving us a basis for rejoicing in the divine action hidden within the world.

This is not to say we can understand each event as purposeful, as a part of a divine strategy, advancing step by step to some utopian ideal. But it is to say that one can have confidence to deny Macbeth's assertion that life is "a tale/Told by an idiot, full of sound and fury,/Signifying nothing."[3] The use of time and space is meaningful because God uses it to do His will. In this sense worship reintroduces us to the world but on a deeper level than we normally experience it.

In various ways, the forms of worship explicitly thrust us out into encounter with the world. This is particularly true of those parts of worship that are free in form, especially preaching and prayer for others, often called intercessory prayer. The texts of hymns, psalms, lessons, creeds, and many kinds of prayer are more or less fixed. But one would hardly expect to hear the same sermon each Sunday and in many parts of Christendom the prayers are not fixed. In these areas it is most easy to understand worship as an encounter with what is going on in the world.

[3]*Macbeth*, V, v, 26–8.

Preaching by its very nature speaks to man with an immediacy deliberately and consciously sought. It seeks to be both fully relevant and also authentically true to the Christian understanding of God's actions. There is the danger that preaching too consciously oriented to "life situations" may fall short of the real depth of authenticity. On the other hand, the preacher risks becoming too abstruse in communicating the biblical message and losing contact with what is appropriate for the lives of his hearers. Preaching is a risk that the Church takes. The preacher never knows when his words become the means of Christ's action for the listening congregation. But one goes on preaching, trusting that his feeble utterances are made strong in the lives of his hearers by the power of God. Preaching, we trust, can be "the power of God unto Salvation," but it is the power of God that makes it strong, not the preacher's. In this sense one ought to speak of preaching as miraculous, as the transformation of sound waves into the action of Christ.

Intercessory prayer is the most obviously worldly part of worship. Such prayer has the ability to encompass all men everywhere. It is not limited by our own personal contacts and acquaintances. The prayer of the Church brings into our lives the situations and conditions of those like us and also those who are not like us. There is, to be sure, a subtle temptation to pray for those who are like us more than for those who are different. During World War II we were more apt to pray for the American forces than for the German or Japanese. But as Christians we are called to pray for all men, to show "benevolence to being in general," though naturally we would submit different petitions for varying circumstances.

The concerns of the Church are the concerns of all men.

I remember once hearing a minister ask, while he was preparing the intercessions for a service of worship, "Are there any concerns of the Church today?" What a strange question! As long as men suffer, as long as men are deprived, as long as men grieve, there are concerns of the Church. And prayer brings these concerns into our lives. Here God is working, bringing us into contact with the needs of our fellow creatures. Intercessory prayer is one way we have to express our concern for others. We reach out to the sick, the bereaved, the lonely, the destitute, and also to those who rejoice.

Worship sends us forth to serve the God whom we encounter both in the cult and in the world. The parting blessing is not a prayer that God might go with us but a declaration that He will keep our "hearts and minds in the knowledge and love of God" and that He remains with us always. The benediction is the proclamation of the gospel as much as any part of the service. It is no accident that the ancient ending of the Roman mass says: "Go." One goes forth into the world to continue the response begun in worship.

The presentation of our "bodies as a living sacrifice, holy and acceptable to God" that St. Paul calls our "spiritual worship" is initiated in worship but by no means ended there. Our rediscovery of our servanthood, begun in worship, is realized in our living throughout the week. In this sense worship grasps our whole future as well as the past. The deliberate encounter with God in worship prepares me for the anonymous God whom I meet in the least of my associates during the week ahead. Offering my service of worship prepares me to offer my service of help to my neighbor throughout my tomorrows.

It is surprising that designs for church buildings give

so little attention to the sending forth of the congregation in mission to the world. We are careful to plan our buildings so as to invite people in. But the mission of the church to the world is scarcely expressed. The dismissal, the going forth to serve, is a vital part of worship.

Worship begins in the church building but continues in the world outside. What we have done enclosed by these walls makes it possible to live in the world outside in a deeper sense. Worship breaks the continuity of our normal consciousness of the world so we can re-enter the world at a deeper level than before. We must do away with any sense of otherworldliness, of unreality, of a spiritualistic mystique in worship when it conceals from us the worldliness of worship. The most important thing we learn at worship is what it is to be God's people in His world.

There are countless areas in which worship affects our life. We will address ourselves here only to two cases: social concerns and evangelism. Basically they are one and the same—elements of Christian mission. But in the thinking of most Christians, social concerns and evangelism are separate activities. I do not like this particular distinction but for convenience will use it here. Service of my neighbor is service of God whether I name the name of Christ or not. But for better or worse, separate commissions, boards, and seminary departments have traditionally concerned themselves with social concerns and evangelism. In our neatly compartmentalized church life, both activities are usually considered completely separate from worship. When they are brought together it is often in a most superficial way, as if one could bend worship into whipping up enthusiasm for some different activity. Our concern here is with two "religious" activities, but it should be understood that worship relates to all our activities in the world and not just church-sponsored ones. Social concerns and evangelism are prime activities of the Church, and we shall investigate the way in which they are bound up with worship.

II

As we have said, worship helps us recover our awareness that God is acting in the world around us. But it is not enough to end there. In worship we come to realize, though we knew it already, that our relation to God is at one with our relation to our fellow men. The ancient kiss of peace was a stylization of the text: "So if you are offering your gift at the altar, and there remember that your brother has something against you, . . . first be reconciled to your brother, and then come and offer your gift" (Matthew 5:23–24). Our relation to God depends upon our relation to our brother. The kiss of peace was a ritual way of reminding us of this fact. This particular action may be too archaic to revive today but the insight certainly is not.

The vertical (man-God) relationship is intertwined with the horizontal (man-man). This is the point of the last judgment parable in Matthew 25:31–46. Those who serve the "least of these my brethren" are in fact serving Christ. Christian worship by its very social nature reinforces this understanding. I come to worship God and I meet my neighbor. Christian worship is as intensely social as any known. And this is why those hymns that mention "my God" are dangerous. Rather we worship the "Lord and Father of mankind." We are reminded of John Wesley's statement that "Christianity is essentially a social religion . . . to turn it into a solitary religion, is indeed to destroy it."[4]

Secondly, Christian worship helps us to understand that there is no Godless sector of life. As we have seen already, God is at work in both the orders of creation and structures of society. In a sense the term "secular" is useless, since all depends upon God. "Secular" is only employed when one limits a small sector of life to the so-called "sacred" and another adjective must be found for the rest. Actually the sacred and the secular coincide, and any effort to make an absolute distinction between the two is bound to incur great difficulties. Paul Tillich tells us: "Everything is secular and every secular thing is potentially religious."[5] The real disjunction comes between created and fallen; sin remains a part of our life. The Cross is not simply a past event, for God's suffering is not done. He relates to men wherever they are.

We like to erect a boundary between sacred and secular, allotting some concerns to religion and conceding the others to the world. But this is unreal. We could learn this from W. B. Yeats who, though not an orthodox Christian, often reveals distinctly Christian insights. In "Crazy Jane Talks with the Bishop," Yeats says:

> "Fair and foul are near of kin,"
>
> . . . .
>
> "But Love has pitched his mansion in
> The place of excrement."[6]

[4]"Sermon on the Mount-IV," *Sermons on Several Occasions* (London: Epworth Press, 1956), p. 237.

[5]*The Protestant Era* (Chicago: University of Chicago Press, 1963), pp. 174–5.

[6]*The Collected Poems of W. B. Yeats* (New York: Macmillan, 1952), pp. 254–5.

The presence of the world in worship reminds us that "fair and foul" have much in common, namely the presence of the eternal and infinite in the temporal and finite. "Eternity shut in a span," Richard Crashaw called it,[7] the incarnation is the story of God becoming a servant.

It is very easy to forget this. We want to keep religion, and especially worship, on a high pedestal, lifted up above the din and smoke of the world. But Christ is always showing up in a manger, talking with prostitutes, riding a lowly donkey, or dying in public. Most of us wouldn't be caught dead talking to corrupt public officials and prostitutes. Christ said they would enter the kingdom of heaven before many of the righteous. Both "fair and foul" are part of the world for which Christ died. "No man," Bonhoeffer reminds us, "has the mission to overleap the world and make it into the kingdom of God."[8]

"What does politics have to do with worship?," some may ask. "A great deal," we may reply. Our realization of the nature of our relation to God and to our fellow man means that politics is intimitely affected by worship. My precinct and my district become part of that world I am given in the Lord's body in holy communion. I cannot regard myself as one with Him and the other worshipers without realizing my responsibility for my neighbors. I offer this sin-stained world of politics in the eucharist and am given back the same world, but now I understand it to be Christ's world. It is the same world but transformed. I understand that I serve God in the foul and in the fair; indeed it is not always clear which is which. The body politic becomes a part of the body of Christ as surely as does the Church.

[7]"In the Holy Nativity of Our Lord God."
[8]*Ethics*, p. 232.

Worship affects the rest of our lives too. Take, for example, our sexuality. What does worship have to do with that? Quite a bit, actually, though the liturgies express it scarcely at all. The Christian liturgical tradition is certainly a celibate one. In worship one understands the nature of his being in relation to others as part of the context of his relation to God. We sometimes act as if sex were something we put over on God. Actually it was His idea in the first place. Genesis makes that quite clear: "Male and female he created them, . . . and God said to them, 'Be fruitful and multiply' " (1:27–28). Sex is part of God's created order, a pretty basic part at that. One receives sexuality as a gracious gift and comes to understand it as such. It is part of the goodness of God's creating acts.

The Church of England's wedding service still contains the words: "With this Ring I thee wed, with my body I thee worship, and with all my worldly goods I thee endow: In the Name of the Father, and of the Son, and of the Holy Ghost." That is a curious phrase, "with my body I thee worship," but it is a pity American revisers ever dropped it. It means to give honor and allegiance to another through one's body. Sex is a means of expressing the worth of another person, one's mate. One serves God by using his sexual nature responsibly, just as in using any other part of creation. Worship reinforces this understanding of our use of the created order.

There is no denying that all too often Christian worship fails to reflect in any clear form our responsibility to society and to other individuals. Too often the forms of our worship are narrow and introverted. We pray for the peace of Jerusalem regularly, but when it comes to praying for the peace of the rest of mankind we hesitate. There is a great need for our forms of worship to relate to the life about us as effectively as they do to past history. Certainly our forms of worship ought to shed their celibate garments in order to reflect more nearly life as lived in families and other societies.

Previously we have mentioned worship's role in formation. To be sure, worship is only one part of our formation as Christians. Education, social activities, counseling, and many other contacts are a part of one's Christian formation. But worship is certainly a vital one, and in this area it has a great deal to do with one's involvement in social concerns.

In the first place, worship constantly rehearses for us the nature of sin. This basic fact of human life is reiterated in most services of worship. One comes to know himself as sinner. But what is more important, one comes to confess the fact that he is a sharer in the sin of the various communities in which he lives. "We have erred and strayed . . . we have offended." I am a sinner, yes, but I also participate in the corporate sin of the Church, of the community, of the nation, as a member of these societies. Even the ultrapatriotic slogan, "our country, right or wrong," acknowledges that one's country can sanction and do wrong. This is true of the congregation that discriminates against minorities or competes with others in erecting magnificent buildings. But it is important that it is the Church, and sometimes only the Church, that acknowledges "We have offended." All men live under sin but it is the worshiping Church that publicly confesses this whenever it assembles to worship.

The second way in which worship forms us as a socially concerned people is in making us aware of our responsibility to "all sorts and conditions of men." Worship expands the frontiers of our lives. We are apt to forget the walls that money builds around us. As we become more affluent we eat in restaurants where the prices are higher and fewer people eat. We go from the lunch counter to the fancier coffee shop and then, perhaps, beyond. Each move separates us from more people. Worship, when the forms are appropriate, can take us beyond the narrow bonds of our daily life to a lively concern for "being in general," for all mankind.

But the message lies deeper than in simply reminding us of the narrowness of our own experience of life. In Christian worship we are made to understand our oneness with others. Many have found the breaking of bread a most meaningful act in holy communion. St. Paul's phrase, "Because there is one bread, we who are many are one body, for we all partake of the one bread" (I Corinthians 10:17), gives us the basis of this unity. It is not human gregariousness, the warm-hearted friendliness of the Church. No, if that were all the Rotary Club would do a good deal better. The oneness of which St. Paul speaks is that which is given by Christ. We are one with each other because we have been given unity by sharing in Christ. The holy communion becomes a symbol of this. A very ancient prayer compares it to the gathering of the wheat "scattered over the hills" to become one loaf.[9] Our oneness derives from participation in that which is far greater than us either individually or collectively, namely Christ. The distinctive feature of the Church is its unity in Christ.[10]

This same oneness helps us see in another sense our

[9]Didache," *Early Christian Fathers,* edited by Cyril C. Richardson (Philadelphia: Westminster Press, 1953), p. 175.

[10]Cf. W. Stählin, "Koinonia and Worship," *Studia Liturgica* I (1964), 220–27.

unity with regard to the rest of mankind. At the same time that we are one in Christ, we are also sharers in the various communities of mankind. It would be a terrible scandal if the sense of our oneness in Christ should blind us to our oneness with our fellow men. We realize, of course, that Christ died for those outside the Church as well as for those within it. Most of us would find it difficult to defend a doctrine of limited atonement. Our responsibility extends to all men, not just to those safely corralled within the fold of the Church.

Worship calls to our mind the responsibility that we assume for all mankind. It is not simply confined to those within the Church, though it is especially focused there. Baptism can be called the sacrament of integration, since it reminds us that we cannot discriminate against those who are incorporated into the Church of Christ without repudiating our baptism. At the same time, worship reminds us that we are indeed our brother's keeper and that we cannot avoid our responsibility to our brother, no matter what his situation. We are one with both the Church and all mankind because of our sharing in Christ.

In the third sense, worship enables us to act as servants of mankind. We should understand that it does not usually teach us how to react responsibly to that which is happening about us. Worship does not replace education and study as training for social action, nor does it take the place of thought and reflection, though some of these may be stirred by preaching. And preaching certainly gives us incentive to fulfill our servant ministry. By and large, worship does not give us the how of relating to our social circumstances. That part of our formation comes through other activities of the Church and our own decision-making.

But worship does enable us to understand ourselves as servants of others. When we gather to celebrate the work of one who took "the form of a servant" (Philippians 2:7), we come to understand what is to be our role in the world. We do not learn the form that our servanthood is to take, but we do come to understand that it is service that is demanded from us. It is perhaps not by accident that the word we use for worship, in English as in Greek, service or *latreia,* can be used in another sense as performing a service for a person.[11] Business firms use the same word. And quite rightly so, for though their end may be financial gain, they do it by being of benefit to others.

Worship helps us to fulfill our calling as servants of Christ and therefore as servants of each other. It means we are enabled to desire what is good for another, though this good-forness may vary from individual to individual. Our life in Christ means that we are constantly being formed to exercise our servanthood. Especially in worship we are called upon to offer ourselves in service. It is not service in churchly vocations, but in serving others in every walk of life as we meet them. Worship, then, calls us to confess, reminds us of our responsibility to others, and moves us to offer ourselves as servants to fulfill the needs of those about us.

III

Worship prepares us for evangelism. Here we find a serious problem in the modern Church. Many people have identified evangelism with revivalistic practices, forgetting that any means of calling men to obedience in Christ is evangelism. For them, evangelism still remains an alterna-

[11]Compare John 16:2 and Hebrews 9:1.

tive to ordered worship. I once heard a clergyman thank God that his denomination was not "deceived by liturgy." I am not sure how the Almighty received this bit of gratitude, though I expect a considerable number of Protestants would have murmured "amen" to it. To many Protestants a fervent zeal for evangelism is still the opposite of a supposedly cold and lifeless interest in worship.

There are grounds for this prejudice. Too often those especially concerned with worship have treated it as an opportunity to indulge in aesthetic and antiquarian interests. When worship was reduced to a question of putting candles on an altar-table or wearing a robe, it was understandable why many scoffed. In our time there have been those who were concerned with enriching services with tidbits dredged up from the past or in producing a "spiritual" atmosphere. Too often worship could become a refuge from contact with the contemporary world.

But those who scorn the irrelevance of some liturgical enthusiasts are not free from problems themselves. It would seem that the chief difficulty in traditional evangelism today is very similar to a basic problem of all Christian worship: professionalism. Vast numbers of modern Christians think evangelism is a good thing—for ministers and priests to do. It hardly seems to occur to the average layman that evangelism is his job, especially his job.

Historically this situation stems largely from a development of nineteenth-century America, where one of the most fantastically successful forms of evangelism ever used was shaped into a system. This is known as the revival system. To it belongs the chief credit for changing the American frontier from an almost completely unevangelized field to a very fertile area of growth for the Church. The method was almost completely clerical, and evangelism was done largely, though not exclusively, through preaching. At that time most of the population lived in small towns, and the minister could and frequently did reach everyone in his community. Everyone went to the county fair and to the revival, sometimes for identical reasons. Both provided excitement and social occasions, neither of which was likely to be overly abundant in a small town. The fair provided entertainment; at the revival the minister could help them get religion. Evangelism was the minister's business.

Contrast that with the present situation. The major part of our population lives in large cities, and within the cities people are constantly moving about. In many apartment buildings it is almost physically impossible for ministers to visit people. Uninvited persons are simply excluded. This does not mean the city dweller is cut off from contacts with other persons; indeed he is given a wider choice of those with whom to associate.[12] But it does mean that no longer is evangelism something that can be delegated to the minister.

In my own community, one of the most religious (statistically, at least) in the country, there are about four hundred unchurched people for every clergyman. It is impossible for the clergy to reach all these people. To the clergy they are no longer accessible. But Christian laymen meet them daily.

Theologically there is good reason for reconsidering the role of the laity in evangelism. The laity, after all, are the Church. What they do or do not do makes the Church. Too often we have acted as if the Church were the minister's business.

12Cf. Harvey Cox, *The Secular City* (New York: Macmillan, 1965), pp. 40 ff.

We have worried aloud a great deal about our double standard in morality. Laymen use strong language and drink but are often shocked if their minister uses either. A layman once told me he thought it would be good for ministers to hear swearing occasionally so they would know what it sounded like. I did not have the heart to tell him I had once worked as a woodchopper and probably knew the subject better than he did.

We are beginning to be bothered by such a double standard of morality. We should be more troubled by our double standard of evangelism. Certainly it is far more important to overcome this double standard of evangelism than taboos on smoking and swearing.

Evangelism is as much the business of the laity as it is of the clergy. Indeed perhaps even more so, since the laity have access to apartment dwellers, fellow workers, and many whom the clergy never reach. To be a Christian is to be an evangelist, and every church is a mission station. Until we overcome our double standards that leave the husk of morality and the entirety of evangelism to the ministers, we are still back in the nineteenth century while the rest of the world is in the twentieth.

What then does worship have to do with evangelism? I would like to suggest that the roots for evangelism in our time lie in new understandings of worship.

We have spoken already of worship as a part of one's formation as a Christain. One is constantly undergoing formation with regard to many separate aspects of his life, ranging from his buying habits to his literary tastes. Many agencies of our culture seek to form us in various ways, some quite antithetical. Christianity forms us by creating a basic stance on life, a style of living for us. It does this in various ways. Biblical and theological study, social contacts with other church members, participation in the various forms of ecclesiastical housekeeping, involvement in the social concerns of the Church, all these are part of the formation of a Christian. But perhaps the most important of all occurs in one's formation by worship.

This is not the primary purpose of worship. The motivations for worship we have discussed previously. Formation is a consequence of worship. It may enter into the motivation, but this is not necessarily so. More often than not, the formation that goes on in worship is not a deliberate or conscious matter. That worship helps form the Christian, however, seems hard to deny and must be taken seriously. In simplest form: Most of us are the type of Christians we are because of the way worship and other elements of Church life have formed us.

How then does worship form us, and especially how does it form us with regard to evangelism? Basically the answer lies in our coming to appropriate for ourselves the acts by which God has made Himself known both in the past and in our own time. Worship gives us these events to hold for our own. In other words, worship makes the Church's memories autobiographical. These events, which we can and should study and discuss with detachment in education, become for us in worship intensely personal experiences. In worship we gain our history. The community's understanding of certain events as revealing the nature of God is an interesting matter for discussion in the process of Christian education. But the realization that these God-man actions powerfully affect my life seems to be largely a by-product of worship.

Through reciting these events and through praising God because of them, we come to accept the events of salvation history into our own lives. To say "Christ died" and to say "Christ died for me" are two entirely different matters. In worship we affirm the latter and respond to such a statement with praise. There is a difference between the classroom and the chapel. Both are vital in Christian formation, but they function differently.

One of the keynotes of worship is the element of repetition. Through the constant rehearsal of past events of salvation as well as representations of God's present activity, these events are assimilated into our lives. It is not strange that the renewed interest in worship in our time (in both Protestantism and Roman Catholicism) has seemed to revolve around both biblical studies and sensitivity to social issues. The biblical reiteration of God's acts for His people is recognized as of capital importance for worship, where the constant repetition of these same events makes it possible for them to become ours. Calvary has meaning for my life because what was done at that time and place is offered to me over and over again in worship. One's formation as a Christian is never complete. It continues by the constant repeating of the ancient events and by referring us to God's present activity. Again and again I am reminded of God's activity in my own time and of changing ways in which I can understand it.

Worship, then, provides the orderly rehearsal of the events of the past and the structures of the present in which the action of God is made known to us. Because of this constant recital, these events become my events and a part of my life. They transform my being. In similar fashion, the basic problem in evangelism is not doing (as we have been prone to believe) but being. One does not do evangelism; rather one becomes an evangelist. To treat evangelism as simply a technique that one learns is to miss the point. Hence our bad conscience about a double standard of evangelism. And putting a layman in the pulpit on Laymen's Day is to miss the point altogether. It is not by having the laymen do what the minister normally does that one makes them take evangelism seriously, or even shows that what the minister can do the layman can do too. It is often painfully obvious that they cannot. The problem of evangelism is much more complex than this. It is the problem of making people evangelists and not simply making them do evangelistic things. Until we become formed so as to see Christ in our neighbor, it will be hard for our neighbor to see Christ in our life.

Evangelism is a matter of being and it is worship that, to a large measure, forms this being. Worship assists in the formation of the new being in Christ, who alone can witness to the world. Worship serves "to equip God's people for work in his service, to the building up of the body of Christ." (Ephesians 4:12 NEB). In constantly rehearsing and rediscovering what he already is, a recipient of God's loving action, one becomes equipped to live the life of an evangelist in the world.

Worship forms us to be the Church in the world. That is the same as saying it forms us to be evangelists. Through worship we understand ourselves to be forgiven sinners, sent forth to witness in the world. What one does inside the church building affects those outside the edifice. It is in this sense that we can speak meaningfully of "building up of the body of Christ." It is a building up both from within and from without: from within through worship and from without through evangelism. And what goes on without is as vital as what goes on within. The church that does not grow is dead but unlike some trees the church needs to grow on the inside as it grows on the outside. Otherwise there is only a hollow frame, ready to be toppled by a strong wind. What happens on the inside is for what is on the outside. So inextricably are our vertical-horizontal relations to God and neighbor intertwined that in saying that worship exists for the sake of God we are, at the same time, saying that worship exists for the sake of the world.

Each Christian as he goes forth from worship goes forth to be an evangelist. What he has come to be in worship he is at his job, in his home, and at the bowling alleys. As an evangelist, he lives the life of the Church in the world. Scattered about the community, each Christian lives his life as an evangelist. This does not mean that he is pushing a Church line necessarily, though witness may take that form. But it does mean that he is enabled to live more nearly the life intended for man, the life that Christ died to restore. Our term "martyrs" comes from the word for witness (*martys*), those who, by their faithfulness in life unto death, made their faith known in the world. Witness for us is rarely this spectacular, but it does mean actualizing that same faith in the world by the quality of our living.

Evangelism, then, is the responsibility of every Christian, not just the ministers. Worship serves "to equip God's people" by forming them as evangelists. Those who have come through worship to understand themselves and others in God are equipped to scatter in the world as God's witnesses. But they too must gather again and again in order to reform afresh and then go back into the world as evangelists.

V
A WORLDLY SPIRITUALITY

In recent years a new term has been added to the theological vocabulary of many a Protestant: "spirituality." Basically spirituality refers to a Christian stance on life. It is an inclusive term, referring not merely to one's devotional life but to the attitudes and actions that reflect his Christian belief. It is more nearly a descriptive term for a style of living than a synonym for personal devotions. Spirituality describes the wholeness with which a Christian lives his daily life.

Other terms have had their use in the past. "Piety" comes closest to being a synonym, but it has suffered from associations with "pietism" and "pietistic," words that too often smacked of a holier-than-thou attitude and a self-confident moralism. The Methodist phrase, "scriptural Holiness,"[1] might be still an acceptable substitute were we not inclined to restrict the ascription of holiness to God. "Personal devotions," as the term is used today, would seem to be such a restricted concept that we would do better to avoid it.

[1] *Minutes of Several Conversations . . . Composing a Form of Discipline* (Philadelphia: Charles Cist, 1785), p. 4.

We shall speak of spirituality as the attitude with which a Christian responds to life about him. We can compare it to formation. Formation is a process that shapes and molds one's spirituality. Spirituality is the result of formation, though neither is unchanging. Formation is constantly changing our stance on life; our spirituality is by no means a static matter. The manner in which we relate to the world about us shows constant change.

Our concern here is with a worldly spirituality. Both Protestantism and Roman Catholicism have tended to sponsor a spirituality focused on life beyond or outside of the world. Protestantism has tended to speak longingly of "the sweet by and by." Look at the "songs of salvation" in most hymnals to see how remote they often seem from daily life. Jesus calls men "o'er the tumult" of life instead of within it. The spirituality of Roman Catholicism frequently seems based upon the monastic orders instead of the secular clergy. The hours too often seem to reflect a withdrawal from the world in order to cultivate either one's own perfection or that of a limited community. Neither form of spirituality seems to be at home in the world. Both are plagued with a bad conscience about life as it is given to us to live.

This is all a bit strange if we take seriously the world as the sphere of God's activity and the place where He makes Himself known to men. If our basic understanding of the world is founded on the Genesis creation stories, it would seem we would be obligated to accept the giveness of the world. Despite man's sin, the world remains the realm of God's creating and redeeming activity. We are forced to affirm the basic goodness of being if we consider God as acting in, with, and under the world. The world is not something to be shunned for God's sake, but to be responded to in terms of our faith in His work there.

We are called to serve God in the world where our work is strengthened and used by Him in the service of men. A spirituality for our day needs to be a worldly spirituality, not a means of escape from God's world. This is the insight of Luther when he recognized that all Christians are priests to each other "and every one by means of his own worship or office must benefit and serve every other."[2] Luther realized that in doing work that was beneficial to others one was acting as a servant both to God and man. The best kind of vertical relationship to God comes through a horizontal relationship of service to man. A worldly spirituality, however, is not the same as ordinary worldliness, since the former understands man to be called to serve and to respond to what He understands God to be doing in His time. Worldly spirituality is based upon a consciousness of God as acting and of the world as the stage upon which He acts. Both the Actor and the setting receive our attention. Ordinary worldliness dwells upon the scenery but misses the action.

Public worship and spirituality are intimately related. The very motivation for worship may properly be called a part of one's spirituality. At the same time, the formation given in worship helps shape one's spirituality.

This interdependence has not been recognized in many congregations where efforts have been made for liturgical renewal. Liturgical renewal is supported by shallow roots unless it goes hand-in-hand with a deepened spirituality. It is comparatively easy to recognize deficiencies in the rite used by a congregation or a denomination and to

[2]"An Open Letter to the Christian Nobility of the German Nation," *Works of Martin Luther* (Philadelphia: Muhlenberg Press, 1943), II, 69.

rectify them. But to deepen the spirituality of the same group adds great difficulties as well as opportunities. Too often efforts at liturgical renewal have been concerned only with public worship. Not only should such elements of spirituality as personal devotions be regarded as areas for renewal, but one's stance *vis à vis* the world. Encouraging private and family devotions may be one step, but even there we cannot stop. We seek the transformation of all of life.

We cannot treat worship in isolation any longer. It is one segment of the Christian life, a very vital one, but never the exclusive one. Saturday night is just as much a part of one's life in Christ as Sunday morning. Of course, what one does on Sunday morning will influence what he does on Saturday night. But it is just as true that what one does Saturday night will affect his understanding of what he does in church on Sunday morning.

The most successful attempts at Church renewal seem to take as their point of departure the serious rethinking of the entire life of the Christian. In this scheme worship comes to have an important part but it is not treated in isolation. There is a danger in trying to make worship do too much. Liturgical renewal is splendid, but it comes as a part of the complete renewal of the Church and not as a single aspect. It is a part of focusing on the essentials of the Christian life, distinguishing between what is vital and what is unessential in the life of the Church.

Our concern here is with the worldly spirituality that seems to accompany renewal in public worship. There are many topics that could be considered. We shall discuss three areas: intercessory prayer, doxological living, and minding persons in God. Though we are talking about different perspectives, our real concern in this section is with the character of Christian life. We are not dealing with any cloistered virtues but with the whole fabric of life as it is lived and understood by Christians. Furthermore, each of these perspectives reflects and affects public worship. We shall say little here specifically about public worship itself, but it should be understood that it is profoundly affected by Christian spirituality.

I

It might seem at first that prayer is an otherworldly topic. Indeed it has too often been treated as a means of escape from "a world of care." Much of the talk about prayer is a language of escape, just as the words often used in prayer are frequently esoteric and strange. And momentarily, at least, prayer involves a break, a discontinuity in one's normal consciousness. It would seem that prayer is anything but worldly.

This is only a short-sighted view of prayer. Prayer, particularly intercessory prayer, is vital to a worldly spirituality. It provides an important means of understanding both God and the world. Far from being an escape from involvement in the world, prayer can be a prime factor propelling us to develop wider contacts with, and concerns for, our fellow human beings.

Prayer is basically the proclamation of the gospel. We have mentioned Calvin's belief that those who do not pray "are also convicted of unbelief because they distrust the promises."[3] Certainly not all the words of prayer are a proclamation of the gospel for some pervert it quite successfully. But the act of prayer is a proclamation of the gospel. In praying one is asserting that God is worthy of

[3]*Institutes,* III, xx, 13.

one's ultimate trust. It is a pity that some take prayer so casually. There are times when one ought not pray, especially when one prays with reservations. Prayer is a radical trusting, a committing to God of ourselves and our concerns and it ought not be taken lightly. To pray is to assert in the most radical way that God is God. Ernst Fuchs has said "the genuine experiences of faith initially appear less in the content than in the fact that one prays at all."[4]

To pray for others is to affirm a belief in the sufficiency of God for the needs of men. It is to assert that ultimately only One can know and dispose of all that is necessary to life itself. When one prays for others he admits the finitude of his own knowledge and power and enlists the assistance of the Infinite. This, of course, means that he has to realize that God will not answer prayer in any obvious and identifiable sense, but that He will dispose of needs in ways beyond our comprehension. The radical trust called for here is to be able to accept a "no" to our "yes." It is to believe God's grace is sufficient to our need and the needs of others without knowing what form that grace may take. One cannot "call the shots" for God.

Part of our confusion about prayer results from a failure to distinguish the different types of prayer. Our present concern is with prayer of intercession, but there are many other types. Most common of all is prayer of supplication in which one prays for himself and his own needs. It is a type of prayer that can easily become narrow and even selfish. In general we may say that unless the same prayer could readily be prayed for us by others, it ought to be avoided.

[4]"The New Testament and the Hermeneutical Problem," *The New Hermeneutic*, edited by James M. Robinson and John B. Cobb, Jr. (New York: Harper & Row, 1964), p. 121.

Prayer of confession is well known in public worship but also plays a large role in personal devotions. Similarly, prayers of praise belong both to the public and personal dimensions of worship. The same applies to prayer of oblation in which one offers himself or his goods in the service of God. These are only some of the many types of prayer used in worship both private and public.

Intercessory prayer is distinguished by being offered on behalf of others. It is prayer offered to meet the needs of other persons. This applies both to prayer for individuals and for groups. Intercessory prayer reaches out and seeks to serve others than ourselves. All men are the subjects of this form of prayer. In this sense it is the most worldly form of prayer, since it encompasses all humanity in a way other forms of prayer do not. Our entreaties bring us into the life of all the world and bring all the world into our lives. At its most immediate level intercessory prayer is directed to those whom I expect to meet on any given day. In this form it has a specific direction to the explicit needs of those I encounter. I pray for the concrete situations in which I relate to others that I may be used on their behalf.

But this is not enough. The intention of intercessory prayer is perhaps best described by a phrase in the *Book of Common Prayer*: "for all sorts and conditions of men." Such prayer reaches beyond the confines of our daily experience. Most of us meet about the same range of humanity day in and day out. Despite the diversity of people in our metropolitan areas, neighborhoods seem to be segregated in a frightening fashion along levels of income, age, and education. It may prove easier to break down the segregations of race and religion than those other equally artificial barriers. Most commuters see people similar to themselves at the hours they "go in." Retail clerks don't usually lunch with stockbrokers. Despite the cosmopolitan nature of our cities we actually live within restricted areas of experience. This is especially true of many parish churches where we only meet people like ourselves.

Intercessory prayer knows nothing of such limitations. We expect to pray for those who are like us, but intercessory prayer, when taken seriously, demands that we pray for the great mass of humanity that is not like us. This form of prayer makes us reach out in concern for those who are not like us as well as for our own kind. It broadens our horizons of life by bringing into our consciousness "all sorts and conditions" of humanity whom we never meet. Most of us have forgotten the farmer upon whom we nevertheless depend. We never meet the subway driver or the pilot into whose hands we entrust our safety. Yet we do encounter them as persons in intercessory prayer and they become a conscious part of our lives. They cease being mere job-fillers and become human beings through prayer.

In intercessory prayer the reality of the oneness of all men before God becomes apparent. Talk about the brotherhood of man often is little more than a nice sentiment. But translated into terms of common sharers in dependence upon God, we realize how minor are the distinctions we make between fellow children of God. One can hardly pray for others without realizing that the divine benevolence extends to all men. All men are equally children of God and therefore fit subjects for our intercessory prayer.

We tend to be squeamish in our prayers. Though Jesus frequently associated with prostitutes and corrupt public officials, we might ask ourselves when did we last pray for them? How often do we hold before God both the victim of prejudice and the bigot, how often the dope addict and the alcoholic? Do we have a right to banish such persons from our minds simply because they are not like us? Is not our responsibility to hold before God these persons precisely because they are our neighbors every bit as much as Jews and Samaritans once were neighbors in Christ's sight, though bitter enemies in man's practice?

Intercessory prayer, perhaps more often than not, intercedes for people by categories rather than individually. Our range of humanity is limited. How few of the three billion humans we know personally! It is only natural to pray by name for those whom we know. This is our first responsibility. But our work does not end there. We pray for the various categories of mankind and for the conditions of their lives. We pray for medical researchers and laborers in dangerous occupations, as well as for those about to give birth and those who explore outer space. As one bidding prayer invites us to, we pray "for all who travel by land, sea, or air; for all prisoners and captives; for all who are in sickness or sorrow; for all who have fallen into grievous sin; for all who . . . especially need our prayers." That is to say, we reach all mankind through praying for men by categories and conditions.

It is by means of intercessory prayer that we fulfill our responsibility to all being in general. Prayer of this type brings into our lives all humanity and brings us into the life of mankind. In this form of giving of ourselves our servanthood has its beginning. Prayer by no means closes with the final "amen." This is only the beginning of our understanding our responsibility to all men. But it is a very important beginning, for it directs us to universal benevolence and not just towards those who are like us.

This is the only contact we are likely to have with the great mass of mankind. But it is a constant reminder to us of the universality of our mission. Every man is my neighbor and hence the subject of my prayers.

There is also another form of intercessory prayer, and this is directed not towards persons but for the functioning of the orders of nature and society. These are impersonal, but they are areas where God is working. Mankind is constantly affected by both the forces of nature and the social forces of civilized life. These forces demand our concern in prayer because of their power to change the quality of human life or to destroy it altogether.

Man's relation to nature changes radically because of the powers which science has opened to us. The same succession of birth, life, and death remain, but how different they become! Our life span has increased, our mobility has expanded fantastically, and now space will soon not be unfathomable. Yet in all this excitement, we tremble at the possibilities for evil in our new relations to nature. We pray that our new knowledge of conception, our power to control nuclear energy, and our penetration into space may be used to improve the quality of life rather than to destroy it.

We are amazed at the collective power of man. The power to communicate knowledge, to build great projects, to improve the lot of the underfed and impoverished, is also the same power to propagandize, to destroy, and to practice discrimination. The structures of our society are morally ambiguous. And so we pray that power will be used wisely and well. We pray especially for those into whose hands power has been committed that they will use it responsibly on the behalf of others.

Furthermore, we pray that the structures themselves will

be adequate to their callings. This means we pray that the city will fulfill the possibilities of cityhood or that the Church will fulfill the responsibilities of its mission. The first responsibility of Christians in the university is not to pray for the conversion of the university. It is to pray that the university fulfill the nature of its calling, that it be the university. The second responsibility may be to pray that we may serve wisely and well to help it be the university. The same would apply to all other realms of life in which we are a part. We pray that the structures will fulfill their appointed task or that they may be enabled to do so more fittingly.

A few more or less practical matters about intercessory prayer deserve our attention here. The plea of the disciples, "Lord, teach us to pray" (Luke 11:1), should remind us of the difficulties of prayer. The disciples, after all, were not newcomers to prayer. They had been devout Jews all their lives, schooled in prayer from childhood. Their request is ours too. We need to learn how to pray. And anyone who writes on the topic must feel something like a hypocrite, as if he had mastered what even the disciples had failed to achieve. The first thing we need to know about prayer is its difficulty. We are constantly in need of learning more about how to pray even while practicing it. Most of us must admit ourselves novices in prayer no matter how long we have prayed.

The where of prayer deserves some attention. Most of us have acted as if prayer were something to be done in retirement, at the moment when we were away from people. Much of this has been based upon a misunderstanding of Matthew 6:6, in which Jesus suggests that the place for prayer is alone in one's innermost room (*tamieion*) or "closet" (KJV)—which does sound a bit stuffy. The point of His comment, however, is directed against hypocrisy. Prayer in the first century was usually aloud. The same was true of reading. Even as late as the fourth century, St. Augustine was amazed to discover Bishop Ambrose reading so that only his lips were moving.[5] In the first century, praying in public was apt to be ostentatious for all could hear a person when he prayed. This is not so in our own time. Most of us pray in silence and there is little danger of being conspicuous or hypocritical.

I would like to suggest that seeking retirement and seclusion for prayer in our own time is unnecessary and misleading. The place for prayer is in the midst of people, both when confronted with individuals and with groups. Indeed, some of the most crowded spots are appropriate for prayer. Think how many people's lives brush against our own on the commuter train. Here we are called to pray not only for our fellow passengers but for those who manage and operate the railway. (Admittedly on some lines this is a bit hard to do.) At the ball game, in the cafeteria, or while driving through the countryside we are made aware of those for whom we are called to intercede. The same is true of any experience that exposes us to the conditions of others. One of the best occasions for intercessory prayer is while reading the newspaper. There one is opened to the lives of countless others, often in conditions of need. Reading the paper may be the most religious act most of us do each day. It may bring us into contact with more people than any other activity. In every area of life we develop sensitivity to the needs and life

[5] *Confessions*, vi, 3.

before God of those about us. Contacts with people expand our life of prayer and prayer increases our sensitivity to the needs of others.

Our horizons for prayer are also broadened by the use of collections of prayers. Our experience of life is greatly enlarged through praying the prayers of others. Especially valuable are the contemporary collections by Michel Quoist, David Head, and Malcolm Boyd.[6]

I have some real doubts about the propriety of prayer offered in the first person singular. There may be an exception in the case of prayer of confession in which I ask forgiveness and help for those matters in which I am solely responsible. But in almost every other area, one ought to take seriously the need to pray in first person plural. We pray with others to praise, to offer ourselves, to intercede. If our prayer could not be conceived in first person plural, it is well to reconsider if it ought to be offered at all. Prayer is not a private enterprise. It is the joining of many voices. When we can join orally with another it is a help in realizing this. But even when this is not possible, we ought always to realize that our prayer is not isolated but a joint venture.

One ought also to ask what does prayer do to us? Let us not try to be too holy in insisting that it is offered to God and we ought to be oblivious of the consequences upon us. Prayer does affect us and we might as well acknowledge it. It affects us particularly in our understanding of the world about us and our relation to it. Prayer, particularly intercessory prayer, leads us to see all men and all orders of life as standing under both the love and judgment of

[6]Michel Quoist, *Prayers* (New York: Sheed and Ward, 1963); David Head, *He Sent Leanness* (New York: Macmillan, 1959); Malcolm Boyd, *Are You Running with Me, Jesus?* (New York: Holt, Rinehart, & Winston, 1965).

God. Such prayer shows us there is no neutral corner of life but that all men and all things stand before the Almighty. One soon learns that intercessory prayer broadens the dimensions of our own lives in extending our consciousness to the needs of others. Even those whom we never meet become a part of our lives.

At the same time, we are made to realize our responsibility to them. Prayer is not a form of auto-suggestion, but it is unrealistic to imagine that it has no effect upon the one who prays. It gives him a deeper and fuller understanding of his servanthood. As his prayer reaches out to all men, so his relations to others change. One cannot pray for others without finding himself acting differently for them too. Prayer widens our concerns and thereby directly affects our day by day living.

II

Doxological living is a broader term than intercessory prayer, since it refers to the cultivation of an attitude of living rather than a specific activity. "Doxological" comes from *doxa* and *legō,* Greek words for praise and speak. We shall define "doxological living" as the possibility of receiving life and acting in it with a mind to the glory of God. It has its beginning in worship but becomes a means of continuing one's worship through his daily living. It is worship become life.

In worship we stand aside from our normal consciousness momentarily in order to reconsider and respond to God. It is in this time of recollection that we rediscover that all we have is God-given. This we knew already, but it had been obscured in our normal consciousness. Worship makes us realize anew what we already knew. Life itself appears in its true nature as a gift from God. We stand closer to the nature of our being in the moment of worship.

It is no wonder that so much of our worship takes the form of thanksgiving. The chief service of Christendom, the eucharist, acknowledges this by its very name. Hardly any kind of worship fails to return thanks to God for what He has done and continues to do. Indeed the basic response in worship seems to be directed by gratitude. If God has done all these things surely we ought to return thanks. In minute form we do the same thing in the blessing before a meal, though here sometimes it demands hope as well as faith.

There is little distinction between thanksgiving and praise. In both Jewish and Christian worship they fade imperceptibly into each other. The offering of thanksgiving to God "for all thy goodness and loving-kindness to us, and to all men" is almost inevitably directed so that "we show forth thy praise." Again, it is "meet, right, and our bounden duty" to "give thanks" and consequently "we laud and magnify thy glorious Name; evermore praising thee." If we start by thanking God for what He has done, we end by praising Him for His goodness in doing it. We can hardly exceed the *Gloria in excelsis*: "We give thanks to thee for thy great glory." Both thanksgiving and praise are based upon what God has done, does, and will do, not upon abstract qualities. It is no wonder that traditionally the reading of scripture lessons has been interspersed with psalms. We respond to the recital of what God has done with our exclamations of praise and thanksgiving.

Our response of praise can hardly end with worship. We glorify God verbally in our worship. The great eucharistic prayer in the *Book of Common Prayer* begins: "All glory be to thee, Almighty God, our heavenly Father, for that thou. . . ." In other parts of our worship we exclaim our praises in glorifying His name by prayers, psalms, and hymns. But this verbal praise is only one possibility. Doxological living is the overflowing of the praise begun in worship into all of one's activities. The Jesuit motto, *Ad majorem Dei gloriam* ("To the greater glory of God"), applies not just to worship but to all of life. We need to learn to live so that all that we do is done to the greater glory of God. All that we do we are called to do to the glory of God. One earns a living, rears a family, votes, and takes his recreation to the glory of God.

We respond to the goodness of God not only in worship but by living to the glory of His name. Life becomes a form of living praise, far more important than the brief moments of worship. One receives life with joy and responds in praise. Thus our living becomes our means of meeting God. Perhaps we can make this more clear by looking at several different areas of life in which the possibility of doxological living is present.

The lives of most of us today are filled with the abundance of our possessions. But does this necessarily mean "the world is too much with us?" What is the Christian use of things? Does it mean an otherworldly asceticism? There is not much chance of that for most middle class people today, but a lingering sense of guilt for an economy of abundance may plague us. How can one receive these gifts from God's hand and use them responsibly except by returning praise to the giver of them? The problem is not a new one by any means even though our abundance has never been equaled. I Timothy 4:4 suggests: "For everything created by God is good, and nothing is to be rejected if it is received with thanksgiving." Abundance may be abused, to be sure, but when accepted with thanksgiving it will be more likely to be well used.

Doxological living calls for the use of material blessings joyfully with a keen sense of their source. Both Christianity and Judaism bless God for things. The Jew may be reluctant to bless things themselves but has no doubt as to the propriety of blessing God for things. Indeed blessing God for things and giving thanks seem to be synonymous. The joyful use of material gifts gives one all the more reason for offering his praise for them. But things used in this sense are not neutral. They are recognized as gifts and so one responds by using them responsibly rather than as things we deserved.

Furthermore, the enjoyment of them is done without guilt. An ancient rabbinic saying goes to the effect that: "A man will have to give account on the judgment day of every good thing which he might have enjoyed and did not."[7] This is world affirming but in a most reverent sense. One understands physical blessings as not to be used indiscriminately but mindfully of the source from whence they come.

This is especially important in our time when the old Protestant ethic of the responsibility to work is being replaced, in part at least, with a calling to leisure. This does not seem as yet to have had much effect on professional people. But it is quite possible in the future that

[7]G. F. Moore, *Judaism in the First Centuries of the Christian Era* (Cambridge: Harvard University Press, 1927), II, 265.

many people will be free to use much of their time at their own discretion rather than to produce income. How can one use recreation doxologically? It means the thankful use of the great blessing of being given time. One learns to live in this day and to be grateful for it without worrying about tomorrow. Accept this day and give thanks for all the love and beauty that come crowding on the mind in it. Its material blessings and its time are seen in their true light only when accepted with thanksgiving offered to the Giver.

Another area in which we are called to give thanks is in the structures of society. Too often these seem to be only vast impersonal matters, the city, the state, the school system, the Church, and others. At best we are inclined to take these structures for granted and to use them as though they were neutral. It is, of course, easy to have a negative approach to them around income tax time. But we should be more aware of how basically the social structures of life affect not only the possibility of civilized life itself but the quality of it.

How often do we give thanks for the government of our city? We are more inclined to curse it. But a more proper attitude would be that of thankfulness for the urban life it makes possible. The stop-light (which is also a go-light) is only one of the many conventions that make social life a possibility. Behind them all lies the power to organize so that life together is feasible with a minimum of conflicts. More positively than that, our social structures enhance the quality of life. The changes we see in our time can be molded to improve greatly the nature of urban life.

Our use and understanding of these structures is radically transformed when we approach them doxologically. Certainly much is wrong with city governments, but the possibility and actuality of government itself is to be received with thanksgiving. If we approach the structures of society with praise for their being, we are more inclined to take a responsible role in the use and shaping of these same structures. Far from being indifferent, they are gifts that we must use responsibly and thankfully. We praise God for the possibility of these structures and realize our responsibility to respond to Him by using them creatively.

Today almost every aspect of sex is exploited except the doxological. It is unlikely that any age within the Christian era has been so saturated with reminders of sex as has been our time. This is not necessarily bad, but it is unfortunate that we remain so oblivious to the doxological aspect of sex. Certainly there are few parts of the created order that one can be more grateful for than sexuality.

Both Judaism and Christianity affirm the goodness of sex. "In the image of God he created him; male and female he created them" (Genesis 1:27). At times within Judaism celibacy seemed close to blasphemy. But again sex is an ambiguous matter. It can serve to give glory to God or it can deny Him. Our calling, first of all, is to understand our sexuality doxologically, that is, as a gift from God. Then it is to understand the proper use of sex as a means of glorifying God. The ability to say sincerely about sex, as about all else, "Praise God, from whom all blessings flow," puts sex in its true perspective.

One partakes of this great gift in its full joy by praising God for it. One uses sex rightly as a means of glorifying God for the greatness of His created orders. It means both a joyful and responsible use of this important element of His creation.

Basically we are called to live all life to the glory of God, not just these few areas we have mentioned. Doxological living is the effort to understand what God is doing in all areas of life and then to respond by acting to His glory. In this sense worship initiates our way of living but it by no means completes it. Living to the glory of God involves all that we do, not just the so-called religious activities but all moments of life. One enjoys a good dinner to the glory of God just as he helps a neighbor to the same end. He has the ability to receive life and use it to the glorification of God.

Of course this means the ability to accept the unpleasant and tragic aspects of life with confidence just as we do the joyful. It is easy to offer praise for that which is pleasant; much harder is the call to give praise in the midst of travail and conflict. We are not seeking a grim stoical indifference but the faith to "praise my Maker while I've breath." Offering praise is not always easy but it is a constant part of the new life in Christ.

Worship can never be considered in isolation. It is true that worship does consist, to a large degree, in singing the praises of the Almighty. But that is not enough. Our praise is not exhausted in worship. The demand before us is that we continue our praise in life lived outside of public worship. We are called to live to the greater glory of God as well as to express His glory in our public worship.

Each and every action becomes a means of doxological living. In all that we do we have an opportunity to do it to the glory of God. Anything that interferes with this, evil to our neighbor or harm to ourself, is a contradiction of this stance on life. A worldly spirituality demands a continual awareness of the doxological character of our relations with others, with ourselves, and with God. Daily we should live our praise to "God, from whom all blessings flow."

III

Another aspect of a worldly spirituality, that of minding persons in God, is directly connected to intercessory prayer and doxological living. Minding persons in God means relating to others by being constantly mindful that in this relationship one stands in the presence of God. All elements of worldly spirituality depicted here are directly involved in one way or another with the way we relate to people or to the social structures of human life.

There are numerous possible ways of relating to other people. One of the most frequent is the case in which a person becomes a means to an end for us because he can perform a service. There is nothing unnatural about this. To a child a mother is the provider of food before she is the object of love. We depend constantly upon those whom we rarely encounter as persons: the milkman and the mailman being the most obvious examples. When I call in the plumber I certainly don't look for an enduring relationship. In many of our relationships other persons serve some purpose but remain basically impersonal.

The other extreme, of course, is those persons with whom we share our love. Wife, parents, children, and others are in this group. We love and expect their love in return. It is common to all humanity that such relationships are a cell with love at its nucleus.

Without cataloguing the other types of human relationships, I would like to describe a third possibility, that of relating to persons in God. One can relate to others impersonally or intimately in love, or the various degrees in between. But a qualitatively different relationship is that in which one learns to mind others in God.

When we approach others within the context of the love of God it means a transformation of normal relationships. It means that whatever relationship another person plays to us in life has a new quality. Most people will continue to be related to us in the most casual ways for the office they perform. But we come to value them as they stand before God; a new dimension has entered our relationship to them. Those whom we know and love intimately are changed too. We value them not just for themselves but as fellow creatures of God.

Fundamentally, then, our relation to others is transformed because we now acknowledge a third party to these relationships. This is not a change in God but a change in our understanding of human relationships. God is there all along, but only when we come to understand His presence in these relationships do we see through to the true nature of the way in which we relate to others. A transformation of our being comes about because of the deeper insight into the meaning of human relationships.

As we have seen, the beginning of this understanding is made possible by the insights gained in worship. There we come to realize more fully the ultimate dependence of all that exists upon God. But it is constantly realized in our life of action whereby we act and react to the actions of others. We mind others in God because we have come to understand them as standing within the perspective of the divine just as we ourselves do. We have obtained new insight into the nature of being, and it serves to change our acting.

Everyday life is transformed when we glimpse the

divine dimension in our human relationships. When we see others in this aspect it becomes possible to forgive them that we ourselves might be forgiven. The love of others becomes a possibility, even of those who repel us. We understand ourselves as beings loved by God not on any merit that we happen to have. God's love for us is an unmerited love that we have done nothing to earn. We love Him because of His excellencies but He cannot love us for the same reason. His love is regardless, a love of divine nevertheless. He who is worthy of all love loves us not because of any good in us that draws on His love. He loves us because "God is love." It is His nature to love even the unlovable.

The knowledge of God's love makes it possible for us to mind others in God. There is nothing particularly lovable in most of those about us. Stand on any street corner and the prospect of humanity as it passes you is a rather bleak one. But that is not the point. Each person is a creature of God and as such needs to be minded in God. Most of them do not attract our love. Some even repel any inclination to view them with anything more than casual indifference. In and of themselves they certainly do not merit our love. But in and of themselves and God the situation is changed. Here we see they do very definitely deserve to be treated with love, since they, like us, are recipients of the same divine love. It is God's unmerited love for us that makes it possible for us to offer unmerited love to others.

Our relationships to most men are brief and soon past. And yet each relationship offers a possibility for showing forth that love in which we stand. Those I pass on the street are related to me in our common dependence upon the love of God for our very being. I am called upon to mind in God both those who have names to me and those who must remain nameless. Both have this in common: They stand with me under the love and judgment of almighty God.

In these relationships prayer has a definite bearing. Most of the people to whom I relate are nameless persons performing certain offices necessary to the efficiency or comfort of our society. I do not know their names; they do not know mine. And I do not complain about this anonymity. But I can relate to them through intercessory prayer. Here I have the possibility of understanding these persons in the context of the divine. I hold them before God and see them in their true light. It is a momentary matter, a short span of time, but it does give me the model of all my relations with others. I am to live for others as if I were praying for them.

And what is it that I seek in my praying and living for others? Basically it is to bring about what is fitting for them. I am not called to program any special course for their lives. What I am called to seek is their good. My praying and living is to bring about the good-forness of those about me. I do not always do this by specific rules, though they normally give me guidance in what is good in general. I must resist the temptation to make others carbon copies of what is good for me. My servanthood is expressed in seeking the good of others, what is fitting to them in their individual circumstances. I see them as standing before God and must seek their good in that place where they stand.

In this sense, my servanthood is to all being. It is a general servanthood, since all men stand before God. But it is a specific servanthood in that the good of different men is different from that of others. "To each one his own" is not just a principle of justice but of love as well. In "benevolence to being in general," we are always having to qualify our actions in seeking different goods. Sometimes children need to be loved with a spanking, at other times by a hug. Our love is expressed to some people by giving them money and to others by refusing to give them money. It is not the money that matters but the harm or good which it does to the recipient. Being "all things to all men" is the only way to mind them in God.

Our daily living is an expression of our understanding of other persons as existing in God. We do not relate to them in an indifferent fashion as just an "I" and an "it" or a "thou." We relate to them as an "I", God, and an "it," or as "I", God, and "thou." There is always a third party to each relationship, namely God. And this is the party that transforms the relationship from one of indifference to one of concern. To say, "I know you in God" is quite different from saying "I know you." The divine catalyst brings about a completely different reaction between persons. One sees human relationships not as neutral and indifferent matters but as a part of the way we stand before God.

A worldly spirituality, then, consists in a changed way of relating to the world about us. Through our worship we come to a deeper understanding of the nature of things. But insight becomes translated into action as we live each day. We reach out into the lives of others by means of intercessory prayer. We relate to the things of life and all its gifts by a doxological approach to all of life. And we learn to relate to other persons by minding them in God. Here then is the possibility of a new stance on life, a worldly spirituality.

VI

THE SUBSTANCE AND FORMS OF BAPTISM

No forms of worship, whether old or new, will matter much unless the worshiper experiences the substance—the meaning and reality—that the forms are intended to convey. Some people may call for the recovery of old forms, and others are apt to beg for new concoctions. Either approach is simply putting rouge on the cheeks of a corpse unless there is substance to give it life. We cannot separate worship from spirituality. The quality of our whole life pours meaning into our worship. Only tombstones measure life in terms of years. The measure of life comes by the meaning, the perception, the depth at which it is lived. Without insight into the substance, forms of worship are only quaint curiosities.

Baptism is a particularly good example of the meaninglessness of forms when an understanding of the substance is absent. The malaise of baptism is a good mirror of the general crisis in our forms of worship. We shall use baptism as an illustration of a broad spectrum of Christian worship today.

A symbol of how little baptism means today can be seen in the insignificant physical provision made for it in many Protestant churches. A cheap glass bowl or brass basin reflects the present insignificance of this sacrament. And the service of baptism is likely to be a sentimental display of good fellowship and a parading of babies. Such distractions as rosebuds, kisses, and a general display of Christian cuteness are spared those who practice believer's baptism. So bogged down in sentimental additions has baptism become in many churches that it seems to exist more for the gratification of parents than for the showing forth of what Christ has done.

But what do we expect? Such sentimentalizing of the sacrament is the result of blank incomprehension of the substance of baptism. Nature abhors a vacuum. Sermons on the meaning of baptism are rare, classroom discussions of it are infrequent, and the genuine appropriation of baptism as a basis for Christian spirituality even more uncommon. With the substance of baptism left largely to the imagination, it is not surprising that the obvious novelty of the presence of babies in the church should be grasped as the focal point rather than what God does for them in baptism. One membership manual describes infant baptism as a "lovely custom" but hardly manages to say anything more for its retention.

We no longer have time for lovely customs in worship. Either we must get to the substance of worship and then use the forms that express it best or else we must find some better way to spend our Sunday mornings. In the case of baptism there is every reason to be excited when we grasp the substance of this act.

I

The best and most direct way of discovering the substance of baptism is by examining what the New Testament has to say about it. This may be obvious, but the obvious is all too easily overlooked. Investigation of the New Testament accounts will not give us much detail about the actual administration of the sacrament in the first century. Our most detailed passage, Acts 8:36–38, has the crucial verse (37) missing in some ancient manuscripts. Debate continues about the actual method of baptizing in the early Church. (There are half a dozen or more possible ways of administering the water.) The baptismal words, given in Matthew 28:19, quite likely come from a later time. We are somewhat limited in what we can say with certainty about the form of baptism in New Testament practice.

This is not the case, however, with regard to the understanding of the meaning of baptism. There are numerous passages that make direct or indirect reference to the early Church's understanding of baptism.[1] Not all of these are clear by any means, but there is ample material to use in trying to sort out New Testament meanings for baptism.

One of the first things we discover in the New Testament sources is that a single mode of interpretation of baptism will not do. A great deal of our failure to sense the meaning of baptism is due to the reliance on a single interpretation (often that of dedication). We neglect the full range of biblical understanding. No tidy formula will do justice to the New Testament witness on the subject. The Bible uses a multitude of symbols in presenting the sacraments. They are not exhausted by one or two interpretations but lead us onward so that we never touch bottom.

There are numerous possible ways to organize the discussion of the New Testament witness on baptism. I have chosen five prominent modes of understanding. This does

[1]Cf. A. George, *et al.*, *Baptism in the New Testament* (Baltimore: Helicon Press, 1964), pp. 13–22.

not mean that there are only five such modes or that these modes are entirely distinct from each other. There are many ways to slice a loaf of bread, and this seems to be only one of many possible ways to divide this subject. However, these five modes do seem to be among the most important, if not the most important, either in the New Testament or in the subsequent history of the Church. Certainly there is considerable overlapping; baptism is a unity. But each of these modes provides a new perspective for looking at the same object.

Any serious understanding of baptism would have to take seriously five modes of interpretation: relation to Jesus Christ, incorporation into the Church, new birth, forgiveness of sin, and reception of the Holy Spirit.[2] All five must be held in tension. No single view is adequate in isolation. Our first clue to understanding baptism is to realize the need to keep in mind the several dimensions of the same object.

The first and most important mode of the interpretation of baptism in the New Testament is that it brings us into a new relationship to Jesus Christ. St. Paul sums it up in Romans 6:3: "Do you not know that all of us who have been baptized into Christ Jesus were baptized into his death?" He continues: "For if we have been united with him in a death like his, we shall certainly be united with him in a resurrection like his." One participates in Christ through baptism into His death and resurrection.

[2]Other writers would identify them differently. Gilbert Cope would also include: "Ordination into the Royal Priesthood and membership of the People of God (Laity)," "sealing," and "salvation from eschatological doom," *Crisis for Baptism*, edited by Basil S. Moss (London: SCM Press, 1965), pp. 92–4. Rudolf Bultmann adds another interpretation: "the naming of 'the name of the Lord,'" *Theology of the New Testament*, translated by Kendrick Grobel (New York: Scribners, 1951) I, 137.

The same theme reappears in Colossians 2:12: "You were buried with him in baptism, in which you were also raised with him through faith in the working of God, who raised him from the dead." The idea is repeated that baptism conveys to us the death and resurrection of Christ. Symbolically, of course, this reflects the rite itself. One descends to be baptized, entering as it were the grave, being buried with Christ himself. One is raised from the water a sharer in the resurrection, having enacted *for himself* that which Christ did potentially for all men. The baptism of Christ in His suffering on the cross can be considered a general baptism potentially for all men.[3] But what happens at baptism is inescapably individualized. This is *my* baptism, it happens to me personally. Despite the puzzling and unique reference to baptism for the dead (I Corinthians 15:29), baptism has a strong individual character in which the candidate is called by name. Only in the wedding service are we so explicit in worship.

A new relationship is given in which it is set forth for all to witness that what Christ has done was done for the person baptized. For St. Paul this means a real change: "So you also must consider yourselves dead to sin and alive to God in Christ Jesus." (Romans 6:11). One has been united to Christ and His victory over death has been conferred upon us. In this sense we share in what He has done. Baptism does not change what Christ has done. But it does change my perception of it. He acted, and He acted for me.

It would not seem to make a great deal of difference at what age this event occurred. It is once and for all. One lives his life with the sense of being a direct beneficiary

[3]Oscar Cullmann, *Baptism in the New Testament* (London: SCM Press, 1961), pp. 19–20.

of Christ's work. What Christ has done is mine and my baptism testifies to this. Luther could exclaim: "There is no greater comfort on earth than baptism."[4] It signifies an irrevocable relationship to Christ that cannot be supplanted.

As is so often the case, the historic liturgies have seized upon a biblical hint and made it a part of Christian worship. In the earliest surviving fonts, one descended into the font as if into a grave. Indeed, the earliest baptisteries resembled mausolea. One went down into the water, water was poured over his head—just as a handful of dirt was cast upon a corpse—and then one ascended from the grave.[5] Even modern pedestal fonts are sometimes slightly sunken in the pavement of the church so that one symbolically descends and rises with Christ.

Closely related to the concept of a new relationship to Christ is the idea of incorporation into His Church through baptism. One is baptized into Christ and in the same act becomes a part of the body of Christ, the Church. Baptism is often referred to as a part or the entirety of Christian initiation. It is generally acknowledged that one becomes a Church member through baptism.

The vertical relationship in which one is united to Christ inevitably brings a horizontal one in which one is united to his fellow Christians. Here is made emphatically clear the social nature of being in Christ. It is not a solo flight. The one body "has many members, and all the members of the body, though many, are one body" (I Corinthians 12:12). We are named as individuals in bap-

[4]"The Holy and Blessed Sacrament of Baptism," *Luther's Works* (Philadelphia: Muhlenberg Press, 1960), XXXV, 34.

[5]J. G. Davies, *The Architectural Setting of Baptism* (London: Barrie and Rockliff, 1962), p. 26.

tism, but the Church into which we are initiated is a social organism.

St. Paul could hardly have discovered a better symbol than to speak of the Church as a body. "For by one Spirit," he says, "we were all baptized into one body" (I Corinthians 12:13). In several places St. Paul points out how this new body transcends all others with which men had hitherto been identified. Among those "baptized into Christ" there remains "neither Jew nor Greek, there is neither slave nor free, there is neither male nor female; for you are all one in Christ Jesus" (Galatians 3:28). Baptism has made us members of the body of Christ. As with the members of the human body, different ones have different functions. Being a part of the body gives life; amputated limbs cannot survive.

The person who has been baptized comes within the company of "those who were being saved." This does not mean that baptism conveys any guarantee of salvation. But it does mean that a person has been placed where salvation is a possibility. Most of us are Christians primarily because we grew up in the Church. Many of us never knew ourselves to be anything but Christians, a fact underlined by our baptism. Certainly many come to faith without having been baptized. Those who do so become identified with the community of faith through baptism. Those already baptized and those coming to faith both depend heavily upon the faith of the community. Baptism exists for the building up of the Church, and the Church lives to build up the faith of those baptized.

A strong sense of identification with Christ and with other Christians rings through St. Paul's linking of baptism and the body of Christ. Those who have become beneficiaries of the work of Christ now have the things of

Christ in common. Theirs is a communion in holy things. Baptism becomes the form of initiation into this life together in which the things of Christ are shared. Here again Christian oneness is set forth by sharing in the waters of baptism.

Historically baptism as the entrance into the Church has been shown forth by locating the font near the door to the Church building. Even today, one symbolically enters the Church building itself during the course of the Roman Catholic baptismal rite.

The third theme is that of the new birth. It is directly related to union with Christ and incorporation into His Church. The metaphor of new birth provides an interestign parallel to the death and resurrection symbolism of St. Paul. In John 3 there is a discussion between Nicodemus and Jesus over being born anew. Jesus tells Nicodemus: "unless one is born of water and the Spirit, he cannot enter the kingdom of God" (verse 5).

The birth represented in baptism is often referred to as regeneration. The word regeneration (*palingenesia*) appears in Titus 3:5: "He saved us . . . in virtue of his own mercy, by the washing of regeneration and renewal in the Holy Spirit." Theologians have argued over whether baptism effects regeneration or reflects it. The question is most often resolved not on the basis of biblical material but upon the disputants' understanding of the nature of a sacrament.

Other pictures adhere to the image of new birth. Baptism represents an immense qualitative difference in one's being. It stands as the frontier between one's old nature and that same nature fulfilled and transformed into a new creation in Christ. It involves putting one's past behind him, leaving the old Adam behind, and putting on the new. In this sense it can be likened to the putting off of an old garment and putting on a new. Indeed, the word (*enedusasthe*) in Galatians 3:27 ("For as many of you as were baptized into Christ have put on Christ") is a word that refers to the putting on of a garment. The same expression occurs in Romans 13:14. It refers to the immense qualitative change in one's being which baptism involves.

Baptism is a new birth in several dimensions. One is born anew, that is discovers himself to be something that he was not before. In the discussion with Nicodemus rebirth evidently involves the transformation of one's being, the same humanity but under a new allegiance. In every sense except the physical, it conveys a re-creation of one's being. The power of sin is broken, he shakes off the infirmities of the old Adam, and becomes a new creature.

In another sense the image of birth meshes with that of St. Paul's regarding the body of Christ. As one was born into a specific body on his birthday, so in baptism he is born into another specific body, the Church. Both births represent gifts of God, a fact brought out in the service for giving thanks for child birth. One's baptismal birthday represents his birth into the household of faith. And hence in baptism he is only named by his Christian name. The surname of the baptized is "of the Father and of the Son and of the Holy Spirit." In this birth one takes his place in a much larger family than at physical birth. Likewise he gains a vast body, the body of Christ scattered throughout the world.

Traditionally there have been reflections of the concept of new birth in the baptismal liturgy. A most obvious one has been adopted in the design of some recent fonts to resemble a pregnant woman.[6] This is in accord with an ancient concept of the font as the womb of the Church through which new members were born into the Church. About as explicitly sexual as Christian worship ever gets is the rite for the blessing of the font at Easter eve. The paschal candle is allowed to drip into the font then plunged in and prayer offered that all those who are born of the water may share in the body of Christ.[7]

A ceremony of very ancient date involves putting a spotless new garment on those who have just been baptized. Here is a literalizing of the biblical phrase "putting on" of Christ. It is retained among Roman Catholics and has been recovered by some Protestant groups. In this symbolic acting out of the significance of the new birth, the old garments have been shed and the new put on.

The forgiveness of sin provides our fourth group of meanings, many of which are closely related to the image of new birth. Being transferred from the following of the old Adam to the new Adam (Christ) includes release from the power of sin. In I Peter 3:21 it is suggested that there is a parallel between baptism and the deliverance of Noah and family from the flood: "Baptism, which corresponds to this, now saves you, not as a removal of dirt from the body but as an appeal to God for a clear conscience, through the resurrection of Jesus Christ." By means of baptism one hopes to pass from the burden of sin to a clear conscience.

In this sense baptism is the decisive step in putting the

[6]Cf. Joseph Picard, *Modern Church Architecture* (New York: Orion Press, 1962), p. 166.

[7]Gilbert Cope, *Symbolism in Bible and Church* (London: SCM Press, 1959), p. 102.

old allegiances behind one. Just as one is born into the world, so he also leaves behind the fetal stage. The transformation through baptism is suggested in Hebrews 10:22: "with our hearts sprinkled clean from an evil conscience and our bodies washed with pure water."

The symbolism of washing is an inevitable one and this concept of purification undoubtedly was associated with baptism even before the time of Christ. That the early Church was familiar with it is shown in such passages as Acts 22:16: " 'Rise and be baptized, and wash away your sins, calling on his name.' " The baptism of St. John the Baptist was similar in its stress on "a baptism of repentance for the forgiveness of sins" (Mark 1:4). It was a theme that was to have an important history within Christianity. Out of it developed doctrines concerning the forgiveness of original sin and actual sins.

The putting of the past behind one was eloquently stated in the renunciations. These indications of a moral change appear in connection with the baptismal liturgy at least as early as the third century. In the *Apostolic Tradition* of St. Hippolytus, candidates for baptism are asked to renounce Satan's service and his works.[8] The same idea remains in the modern Roman Catholic rite; the candidate or sponsor renounces Satan "and all his works" and "all his allurements" (*pompis*). Other liturgies contain the same renunciations such as "the vain pomp and glory of the world" (American *Book of Common Prayer*).

Numerous exorcisms reflect the same thing. Ancient examples survive, but the modern Roman Catholic rite

[8] *The Treatise on the Apostolic Tradition*, edited by Gregory Dix, O.S.B. (London: S.P.C.K., 1937), p. 34.

shows the same spirit: "I exorcise you, unclean spirit, . . . come forth, depart from this servant of God."[9] The point of these expressions is the deliverance from sin, the forgiveness that since New Testament times has been associated with baptism.

Our fifth topic, the reception of the Holy Spirit, is one of considerable complexity. The relation of water baptism and the gift of the Holy Spirit, so neatly linked in John 3:5, is not so clear in the light of other passages. In some instances, baptism and the reception of the Holy Spirit are directly related. Elsewhere they seem to be altogether separate. Acts 2:38 point to a direct linkage: "Repent, and be baptized every one of you in the name of Jesus Christ for the forgiveness of your sins; and you shall receive the gift of the Holy Spirit." In Acts 10:44–48, it is quite obvious that the "gift of the Holy Spirit had been poured out even on the Gentiles" prior to their baptism, while Acts 8:14–17 records baptized Christians who had not received the Holy Spirit. There is the additional complexity of the gift of the Holy Spirit being associated with the laying on of hands. Further complexities appear in Ephesus where St. Paul meets disciples who have received the baptism of St. John the Baptist but have never heard of the Holy Spirit. St. Paul baptizes them "in the name of the Lord Jesus," and the coming of the Holy Spirit seems to be associated with the laying on of hands (Acts 19:1–7).

The situation is further complicated by the accounts of the baptism of John the Baptist and the statement attributed to him that Jesus "will baptize you with the Holy Spirit and with fire" (Matthew 3:11). Similar statements appear in the other three gospels. They also record

[9] *Collectio Rituum* (Collegeville, Minn.: Liturgical Press, 1964), p. 11.

the descent of the Holy Spirit in the form of a dove on the occasion of the baptism of Jesus. There is abundant evidence of the association of the Holy Spirit with water baptism, even though it is also linked to the laying on of hands.

At any rate, the association of the Holy Spirit with baptism would seem inevitable on other grounds. As we have seen, those who are baptized are placed within the Church that is the locus of the activity of the Holy Spirit. As part of the body of Christ, they stand before the action of the Holy Spirit, at the center of Its activity. Thus to ask whether the Holy Spirit is received at baptism or one merely enters the realm of Its activity seems to be mere quibbling.

There are other metaphors that suggest the gift of the Holy Spirit as by-products of baptism. Chief among these is illumination, or enlightenment. Hebrews 6:4 ("For it is impossible to restore again to repentance those who have once been enlightened") is possibly a reference to baptism. Again, St. Paul connects baptism with being sanctified and justified: "But you were washed, you were sanctified, you were justified in the name of the Lord Jesus Christ and in the Spirit of our God" (I Corinthians 6:11). It would appear that among the gifts of the Holy Spirit received in baptism are illumination, or enlightenment, and the beginning of sanctification.

There have been various ways in which the reception of the Holy Spirit has been shown forth in baptismal liturgies. The dove has been associated with baptism throughout the centuries. As a symbol of the Holy Spirit it recalls the baptism of Jesus and the recurring presence of the Spirit in each baptism. In the Roman Catholic baptismal rite, salt is placed in the mouth of an infant about to be baptized as a symbol of wisdom. A literalizing of the idea of illumination comes in giving a lighted candle to the baptized person at the conclusion of the service. The present Roman Catholic text prefers to stress the element of preparation in this action, alluding to the parable of the ten virgins.

We have seen five different facets of the same jewel. Baptism is not susceptible to a single interpretation. There are at least these five dimensions that ought to be taken seriously in order to get at the substance of this sacrament. It is equally true of many other acts of worship that one has to wrestle with a multitude of interpretations to glimpse the profundity of meaning present.

Throughout the history of the Church, first one and then another mode of understanding baptism has come to the fore. The constant problem has been that of holding the biblical metaphors in the proper tension. Frequently one or the other of them has predominated, obscuring the others. In St. Augustine's writings the concept of sin and its forgiveness seems to predominate in some arguments, while incorporation into the Church looms large in the arguments against the Donatists. Modern Protestantism neglects the biblical witness to the forgiveness of sins in baptism, while incorporation into the Church is treated relatively seriously.

Some current interpretations of baptism simply do not occur in the New Testament. If there had been any reference to the dedication of infants, all the controversy about the baptism of infants would have been avoided. References to infant dedication in baptism are absent from the New Testament. Dedication of infants seems to be a modern idea, and one that might very well be set aside while the richer biblical metaphors are explored with the care they deserve. The substance of baptism is best discovered through a balanced appropriation of the several biblical modes of understanding this sacrament.

II

The special power of baptism is that in this brief ceremony the entire gospel is shown forth. Baptism is the gospel in a nutshell. Unfortunately the evangelical nature of this sacrament is rarely understood. Among Catholics it has been a rather private ceremony. Too often in Protestant worship baptism becomes a trifle at the end of morning worship, a last delay before going home. The English Reformers were perceptive when they required that baptism take place "immediately after the last lesson at Morning prayer"[10] or at the same place in evening prayer. Baptism is part of the proclamation of the Word. What is spoken in the reading of the New Testament lesson is demonstrated in the act of baptizing. Both are means of witnessing to the work of God for His people.

In public baptism we are not only witnesses to the baptism of another but are put in remembrance of our own baptism. Baptism comes home to us because of its intensely personal nature. *I* was baptized, not just people in general. Baptism is recurrent testimony to me that *I* have been accepted. One recalls the famous passage in which Paul Tillich speaks of acceptance: "Do not seek for anything; do not perform anything; do not intend anything. *Simply accept the fact that you are accepted!*"[11] Never is this clearer than at baptism. Whether as a child

[10] *Prayer Books of Edward VI,* p. 394.

[11] *The Shaking of the Foundations* (New York: Scribners, 1948), p. 162.

or as an adult, baptism testifies to me that I have been accepted.

It is this intense personal quality that distinguishes baptism. It happened to me; it was shown to me. Most likely there were witnesses, there may have been a certificate, a document that sometimes even has legal status. This event happened to me, and it was shown to me that I am accepted. Though others may have spoken for me at the time, the event was mine. My name was spoken, and the water was poured upon my head. Baptism clearly addresses me and tells me of my acceptance.

Baptism shows forth the triumph of God's grace. God gives Himself to us in baptism. It is a gift, not something that we work out for ourselves. Above all, it is not a reward for faith. The person baptized is passive, he is baptized. Baptism is not something one does for himself. Baptism comes from beyond us. We are accepted. It is not for us to prove our acceptability, not to demonstrate our merit, not to deserve baptism.

In the case of infants this is all the more apparent. The child comes into this world a helpless creature, totally dependent upon others. It is hard for those who have children to doubt the reality of original sin. The love that parents are privileged to bestow on their offspring is an unmerited love, offered freely before the child is of an age to respond to it. In similar fashion, baptism testifies to us of the love of God before we are able to respond. The child baptized a few weeks after birth is completely passive, sometimes even asleep. But the grace of God is offered freely and fully in the act of baptism.

For the adult, baptism is likewise a gift of God's grace. Unfortunately believer's baptism sometimes seems to suggest that baptism is a reward for belief. This is not the case, for even the believer's faith is a gift itself. There is the danger of believer's baptism becoming a form of works righteousness, as if one could earn the right to be baptized. Baptism is God's work and this ought always be kept in mind. We come to this sacrament passively to have something done for us, something in which God's love triumphs.

In this sense the question of age may be a bit irrelevant. Does it really matter whether infants or only believers are baptized? In either case the act is quickly past. Has this vexing question that has divided Christendom really been worth the conflicts it has caused? In the baptism of infants or the baptism of believing adults, baptism is given by God irrespective of the merits and accomplishments of the candidate. What really matters here is not the faith or anticipated faith of the candidate but the free offer of God's love. Those churches that practice infant baptism today also make provision for the baptism of "such as are of riper years." Would it not be possible within a united Church to allow for both the existence of infant baptism for those who feel it testifies supremely to the unmerited love of God, and baptism of believers for those who insist the candidate must be conscious of what he receives?

In either case, the important matter is in understanding that which is given in baptism. Here we are forced back to reconsidering the biblical metaphors with regard to baptism and their testimony of what is given to us. Above all, it is the love of God that precedes us, bringing us to baptism, and abiding thereafter as a pledge and seal to us that we have been accepted and nothing can separate us from God's love.

The problem of the relation of baptism to confirmation may possibly be approached from this angle. The Reformation tended to associate confirmation with the learning of one's catechism, so that, in effect, it became a means of enforcing church discipline. Worship almost always suffers when it is saddled with the responsibility of being a probation officer. The exclusion of notorious sinners from holy communion might be an effective means of enforcing church discipline (salvation by embarrassment), but the meal spread for sinners should not assume this role. Worship should not be used to police the congregation.

What happens in confirmation is also a gift. Even though one affirms for himself the vows made at his baptism, it is only by power from God that he can do so. Confirmation is not earned any more than baptism. The faith by which one responds is a gift, and the grace given in confirmation is a gift. Making confirmation dependent upon learning one's catechism all too easily gives it the quality of a reward. Confirmation may well underline the passage of a person through a certain stage in life and the fact that God's presence is with him during the period when puberty and growing responsibilities change the nature of his life. But linking confirmation with the learning of doctrine has two bad consequences: It conceals the fact that confirmation is a gift, not a reward, and it also suggests completion of the learning experience at an age when one ought instead to mark the initiation of Christian education on a deeper and more mature level.

If confirmation is a gift like baptism, it may not matter too much when it is given. A gift is a gift at any time, Christmas or otherwise. It may be that the ancient unity of Christian initiation—whereby baptism and the sealing of the Spirit were parts of one and the same ceremony—would have much to recommend itself. The Eastern Orthodox churches have never given up this practice. Baptism and confirmation still go together for these Christians, as for the Church of the third century. The gift comes at one time. It is true that there is a strong witness to the unity of the Church in the presence of the bishop at confirmation. But Orthodox Christians have preserved this sense of unity in other ways and retained the primitive unity of Christian initiation rites. Their example commends itself to serious study by other Christians.

It remains to inquire what is the relation of the baptized person to the world. Too often baptism seems to be an esoteric cultic practice, withdrawing one from contact with the rest of the world. Parallels to Christian baptism abounded in the mystery religions of the early centuries of the Christian era. In these one was initiated into secret societies, existing for the salvation of members but generally indifferent to the rest of the world. Christian baptism stands in sharp contrast to this indifference and withdrawal from the world. Christian baptism prepares one to serve in the world not in any superficial sense but in the dimension of depth. It is propulsion into the world rather than withdrawal from it.

It may not make much sense today to go on reiterating that baptism ordains us into a "royal priesthood." Both words need so much explanation to overcome misapprehensions. "Royal" is archaic, and "priesthood" is dimly religious and somewhat spooky. "Minister" comes out somewhat better, especially as a verb. But best of all is "servanthood." Baptism ordains us into servanthood.

Baptism brings us into a new relationship with Christ in which we share our Lord's servanthood to the world. The Christ to whom we are joined in baptism is the same one who "emptied himself, taking the form of a servant, being born in the likeness of men" (Philippians 2:7). We are baptized into the Suffering Servant, assuming His servanthood and public responsibility in the world.

Baptism gives one to the world through Jesus Christ. If we understand ourselves as commissioned to serve, we sense this even more deeply because of our bond of unity to Him who took the form of a servant. Our relationship to others is changed by our understanding of the world as the place where our servanthood is exercised in every concrete situation in which we live. Paradoxically, one might say that baptism elevates one to the role of a servant. Because Christ has glorified servanthood, we are honored to share in the same role. Thus our union to Him in baptism is at the same time a commissioning to go forth, to serve others, and perhaps to baptize them into the same servanthood.

Perhaps too much has been made of the baptismal renunciation. One renounces Satan and all his works, but the positive aspect, that one must do more than merely renounce evil, does not seem to have lodged itself so clearly in the baptismal liturgies. The Christian calling is not simply the renunciation of evil but the assumption of servanthood. One renounces sloth and indifference in taking up his cross in baptism. But, more importantly, he affirms his role as a servant.

The new life in the Church, inaugurated in baptism, serves to equip one for service in the world. Baptism is strongly individual in its personal testimony to me that I am united to Christ and that what Christ has done is mine. But baptism is also strongly corporate in that what I have in Christ I have in common with my fellow Christians. I may come to baptism alone but I go away from it united to the company of the baptized. The Church—by its common life of worship, study, and work—equips one to fulfill his role as a servant. In worship he comes to reconsider and respond to the nature of things. Study means both learning why one serves and how one serves. Reinhold Niebuhr used to remark that there was quite a difference between being a fool for Christ and being a damn fool. Study involves strategy as well as motivation. And work provides a further means of exercising one's servanthood in mission to others.

One of the most significant aspects of life in the Church is the union of members to one another. Though the body has many members, they are first of all one body. We are united to each other through our common membership in Christ. Therefore we do not go forth to serve alone but in the power of serving together. Being a Christian is not a solitary vocation. Being a Christian means serving in union with others. The term "yokefellow" is a good expression of this aspect of Christian service. At the lowest level, it is simply a matter of morale in knowing that one does not serve alone. To cry with Elijah, "I, even I only, am left; and they seek my life, to take it away" (I Kings 19:14), may be very tempting at times but is not true to life. The Lord may keep His seven thousand well hidden, but one knows that they are there. It is not surprising, however, that the disciples went out two by two (Luke 10:1). At the highest level, one serves because of his consciousness that through Christ he is united to his fellow Christians and together they are called upon to serve all men.

We have previously referred to baptism as the sacrament of integration. The sense of this is that if one is united to Christ in baptism and incorporated into the Church, he can hardly fail to understand his oneness with all the baptized. To discriminate against others because they are not like us in superficial ways is to forget the testimony of baptism: Those who have been baptized are like us in all that matters. They have been accepted by God and who are we to find them unacceptable to us? It is tragic that many Christians have failed to see that baptism provides the strongest possible case for the acceptance of Christians whose skin may be of a different color. Refusal to accept the baptized is a form of blasphemy, a denial that God's activity in baptism has any reality at all.

Even closer to home, for most of us, is the witness of baptism against the divisions of the Church. It can hardly be thought now that baptism will provide a shortcut to Christian union. But it certainly provides a constant reminder of how the divisions within Christendom are in effect a denial of the meaning of this sacrament. Our oneness in Christ and in each other is testified to every time we baptize, even though we do it at different fonts and in different churches. The font ought to be the symbol of unity for all who live in a parish, but instead we have a multiplicity of fonts. Maybe someday one common Christian font can be established in each area. There is no more need for all churches to be baptismal churches today than in ancient times. Our servant ministry is supported by our unity in Christ and each other. We need visible symbols of this oneness.

Baptism enables us to carry out our servanthood in the world. It is like the wedding service, a brief ceremony soon over but changing the character of the rest of our life. The meaning of baptism, like that of marriage, is only fully discovered in daily living in this new condition. It would be a great step in the renewal of the Church if Christians could realize what the substance of baptism involves for life in the world. God gives Himself to us in baptism and our response is to give ourselves in servanthood for others. Baptism makes us aware of the true nature of reality and our entire life, our spirituality, is our response to it.

VII

LOSS AND GAIN

Despite their apparent permanency, the forms of worship reveal constant change. Much more is changing than we may realize, though these changes are not necessarily all improvements. It is our purpose now to look critically at some of the current changes, to see what is being lost and what is being gained.

Professor Massey H. Shepherd, Jr. is, no doubt, right in speaking of a "canon" of Western Christian worship in the same sense that one can speak of a canon of New Testament books.[1] Shepherd states that the four basic ingredients of Christian worship were well established by the end of the sixth century: the eucharist, baptism, the divine office, and the usage of the Christian year. Basically this has remained the center of Christian worship ever since. Though theoretically the "canon" is not closed and new basic types of worship might emerge, there does not seem to be any immediate prospect of this. We shall probably do well to take seriously the permanency of these basic types.

[1] *Worship in Scripture and Tradition,* edited by Massey H. Shepherd, Jr. (New York: Oxford University Press, 1963), p. 163.

Within the central churches of Protestantism the normal diet of worship is provided by the Christian year, the eucharist, baptism, and a service derived either from the divine office or the first portion of the eucharist. To these must be added two occasional services: weddings and funerals. Preaching may or may not be a part of any of these services. The eucharist is observed on a quarterly, monthly, or, increasingly, on a weekly basis. Likewise baptism (and confirmation) are observed frequently. The usual Sunday morning service, curiously enough, lacks a consistent name. Usually it includes hymns, psalms, lessons, prayers, a creed, an offering, and a sermon. Weddings and funerals come as the occasion demands. There does not now seem to be much reason to predict subtractions or additions to this list of hard core services within Protestantism.

It is possible to anticipate more changes in less firmly-established types of services. Most common are three: sacred concerts, the evening service, and prayer meetings. Sacred concerts seem to be on the increase, especially in the large city church with an ample music budget, though there is no prospect of residential choral establishments except perhaps in schools and seminaries. The evening service is a common Protestant type, usually marked by informality. Its death seems imminent in many churches and it may have few mourners. Though it may be dying it is remarkably hard to kill by those so minded. Its place, when not pre-empted altogether by television, would perhaps better be taken by educational groups or by an evening eucharist. Another moribund period piece in many churches is the midweek prayer meeting. Once again, it is probably necessary to let it die before it can be resurrected in another form. Common prayer ought to be a viable part of Protestant church life, but the usual prayer meeting obviously has failed to fill the bill. One possible alternative might be the small group disciplined in a common life of prayer and study. This may indicate the need for vocational or neighborhood groups, meeting to sustain each other. The old prayer meeting had the great merit of congregational participation, but it tended to be ingrown and to lack any sense of discipline. It is difficult to generalize about other services of worship within Protestantism, and obviously these three are subject to great fluctuation within denominations as well as between them.

We are more concerned here with the changes which are under way within the "canon" of services: the Sunday morning service, the eucharist, and baptism. It might not seem that changes are occurring, particularly in those denominations that have not revised prayer books. But this is not the case. The changes come by slow degrees, not by sudden lurches forward (or backward). Morning Prayer in the Church of England has not undergone any official revision since 1662 (and not a great deal then). But there have been tremendous changes in the way the service is done despite the unchanging rubrics. The clerk is now defunct, hymn singing has been introduced, and indeed the tone of the service would seem most strange to a Caroline divine even though the words sounded familiar.

We shall seek to examine these subtle changes. Usually they happened without being recognized as deliberate change. Revisions in official books of worship are widely-heralded events though usually they are *ex post facto,* simply making official changes long desired or actually accomplished. The changes that really matter and that are so difficult to chronicle are largely changes in emphasis. The changes sneak up on us. The increased attention to the sacraments in Protestantism today is of major importance, though exasperatingly difficult to document. Indeed, the hardest question with regard to the history of worship is usually: "When did it begin?" A new emphasis begins discreetly and grows in popularity till suddenly we recognize it with a bit of shock as a *fait accompli.*

Our present purpose is to try to transfix in mid-air some of the current changes in order to analyze them critically. There is nothing necessarily good or bad about changes in the forms of our worship. Roman Catholicism has introduced a number of changes in the forms of the mass and most scholars would greet them with enthusiasm. But each change brings a loss as well as gain. If there be gain in congregational participation, there may at the same time ensue a faint contempt for what becomes too familiar. Change is as ambiguous as it is inevitable.

We shall try to discern some of the most important changes under way in Protestant worship in order to raise questions about loss and gain. There are a number of good things we may be losing, there are other things we could afford to lose, and then there are matters we are, or ought to be, gaining. If we can become more aware of these changes we can approach them critically and try to prevent loss and encourage gain. And in some instances we may conclude that loss and gain are well balanced. At least we ought to try to discern what is happening with regard to worship and to evaluate it. In this way we can apply ourselves to the practical task of the continued reform of Protestant worship.

I

There are a number of good things in Protestant worship that we are losing or may have lost already. It is not always easy to understand the demise of some aspects of worship, though it may be that many things have been lost simply from failure to appreciate them. More often than not, losses come from indifference rather than from deliberate action. It may well be that the history of Christian worship is the history of Christian laziness. The loss of frequent communion in the Middle Ages or the failure of Calvinism to recover it in the sixteenth century should not be blamed entirely upon the clergy or the magistrates. If people had cared enough to make the effort it might have made a difference. Too many things in worship have been sloughed off because of indifference and laziness.

Frequently the losses are so intangible that it is hard to realize something vital is disappearing. Nobody makes a decision for a whole denomination to abandon free prayer. It simply disappears here and there until it has vanished. It goes out, as T. S. Eliot might say, "not with a bang but a whimper." The end of some things we can welcome, but the end of others we ought to mourn or try to prevent.

It is unfortunate that some of the distinctive Protestant contributions to Christian worship are those that seem most threatened within Protestantism today. Ironically, at the same time, some items such as free prayer, congregational singing, and preaching are being increasingly appreciated among Roman Catholics. The Protestant Reformation was, at least in part, a liturgical movement, and it is not surprising that many of the distinctive features of Protestant worship have parallels in the worship of the early Church. It is remarkable that within Protestantism, where these treasures ought to be guarded most carefully, there seems too often to be a tendency toward indifference. We shall look at five threatened areas: freedom in determining the forms of worship, spontaneity in worship, congregational singing, various expressive actions, and preaching.

Freedom in the ordering of worship has long been a cherished heritage in those churches developing out of English Puritanism. The *Westminster Directory for Public Worship* of 1645 would appear to be a representative document. It provided certain "help and furniture" for ministers but entrusted a large amount of freedom to them in ordering worship as they saw fit.[2] This responsibility reflected a disillusionment with the sixteenth-century ideal of uniformity in worship, an ideal that has been tacitly set aside in Anglicanism and seems to be on its way out in Roman Catholicism. Some Puritans, of course, were content with a fixed form of worship provided it could be done on their terms. The Middleburg and Savoy liturgies are examples.[3]

The freedom that the *Westminster Directory* envisioned was not anarchy but the following of basically similar patterns, with details determined locally. It was, in some respects, a return to the second-century practice, recorded by Justin Martyr, of the one presiding at worship, making prayer "to the best of his ability."[4] Essential guide lines were laid down, but for sufficient reason one was allowed to depart from them. This is the principle of Puritan

[2] *Liturgies of the Western Church*, edited by Bard Thompson (Cleveland: Meridian Books, 1961), p. 356.

[3] Ibid. pp. 322 ff. and pp. 385 ff.

[4] "First Apology," *Early Christian Fathers*, edited by Cyril C. Richardson (Philadelphia: Westminster, 1953), p. 287.

worship at its best; one follows a given pattern when possible, but makes changes when he considers them advisable. Thus John Wesley could champion the use of the *Book of Common Prayer,* but for good and sufficient cause would add hymn singing, field preaching, extempore prayer, and even construct whole new services.

It is this reverent pragmatism that seems to be threatened today. With most denominations bringing forth official books of worship, there may prove to be a false security in finding a "correct" way of ordering worship. Uniformity does not have a great deal to commend itself. Freedom in ordering worship has the advantage of using forms best suited for the educational level, the musical ability, and the general background of a congregation. It is a dangerous gift, this freedom in worship, and certainly has led to some atrocious ordering of worship. But it may be worth the risk. We can be most grateful for the new books of worship that point to standards of excellence. But all would not be gain if they were to be slavishly followed with no thought to ordering worship to reflect the sociological conditions of each individual congregation.

A particular case in point is that of free prayer as contrasted to set prayer, that according to fixed forms. A few extreme Puritans even refused to sanction the use of the Lord's Prayer in public worship, taking it only for a model.[5] But free prayer, or as it is better called, extempore prayer (prayer from the time) need not be thought competitive to fixed forms. Unfortunately, there seems to be at present a widespread tendency within Protestantism to give up free prayer altogether in favor of the use of fixed forms.

[5]Horton Davies, *The Worship of the English Puritans* (Westminster: Dacre, 1948), pp. 99 ff.

As so often happens, something can be killed by the abuse of it, even though the use of it is highly beneficial. Luther's principle that the abuse of an item does not take away its use should be remembered. Certainly free prayer has been subject to considerable abuse. Forgotten has been John Wesley's question: "Are not then the words we speak to God to be set in order at least as carefully as those we speak to our fellow worms?"[6] Prayer for the times should not be prayer unprepared. The lack of preparation has tended to kill free prayer. At times free prayer is confused with preaching and becomes mere intellectual nagging of the congregation, though addressed to God. At the same time, it is apt to stretch out to such a length that it becomes difficult for people to follow and appropriate. Too often tedious, repetitious, and narrowly conceived, free prayer in general has become suspect.

We would do well to consider the advantages of free prayer at its best. It has the great advantages of relevancy, immediacy, and the ability to reflect the concerns of the Church at any place or time. How does one pray in a farming community when there is fear the irrigation ditches will run dry, in a city where there are race riots, or during a strike? No set forms can cover all contingencies. The relevancy of free prayer is demanded. Yet it must be prayer done responsibly, that is prepared as carefully as the sermon and based on the minister's pastoral concern for, and knowledge of, his people.

One exception to the general decline of free prayer has been the introduction of what is known as "the concerns of the Church." It might better be known as the concerns of the Church and the world. The practice evidently orig-

[6]John Wesley, *Journal*, edited by Nehemiah Curnock (New York: Eaton and Mains, n.d.), I, 309.

inated in the East Harlem Protestant Parish and has spread from there to a number of other congregations. The intention was to make explicit the relationship between worship and the responsibility of Christians to the world at all times. In practice the concerns of the Church consists of members of the congregation announcing, at a designated point in the service, the needs of others. Minister and congregation then offer prayers of intercession and pledge their services on behalf of those needing help. No better indication of the worldliness of worship can be found than that provided by this particular form.

The ideal practice is the use of both free prayer and set forms. Both have advantages. Set forms bring into use the riches and experiences of the Church throughout time. Many of the prayers of the Roman mass or *Book of Common Prayer* can be traced to the sixth century or earlier. They have proved to have a permanent value because of their scriptural quality, their reflection of the concerns of man, and their concision. Set forms compensate for the narrowness of any individual's experiences. Free forms, however, speak to and for the time. They grow out of a pastor's experience of his people and their concerns. He prays for and with them, putting their concerns into words. In a sense, the pastoral prayer is a summation of all the prayers offered by individuals of the congregation during the past week. We need both set forms in prayer and free prayer at its very best.

Closely related to the area of freedom is that of spontaneity in worship. Even free prayer that is prepared does not have full spontaneity. Indeed, this has been a problem throughout the history of the Church. There has been a recent interest in speaking in tongues in worship. Those who have witnessed this practice will have to concede some points in its favor, however reluctantly they may do so. Speaking in tongues is considered the action of the Holy Spirit witnessing to men in their here and now. It seems to be original and devoid of artifice. There is a directness and immediacy about speaking in tongues that is particularly compelling to the observer.

But the problems were visible to the Church from the start. St. Paul wrote the Corinthians that it was better for him to "speak five words with my mind, in order to instruct others, than ten thousand words in a tongue" (I Corinthians 14:19). The problem of making it possible for others to understand and participate in such worship eventually led to the discarding of this form of worship, and it is perhaps just as well. But speaking in tongues does testify to a desire for spontaneity that we ought to heed. This desire may be a lasting witness to us, though speaking in tongues does not have much to recommend itself to us today.

How does one gain spontaneity in worship, or is it an impossible effort? There are circumstances in which it appears, though most of them seem out of the question for the average church. I have seen people walk up during the sermon in the East Harlem Protestant Parish to place an offering on the altar-table. This just could not happen in most churches. No theological objections could be raised, but it is contrary to the formality with which we surround our worship. It is a pity that the fervent "amen" during preaching has died out, a victim of our self-consciousness. Yet liturgically it was an excellent act of congregational affirmation of the Word. Totally unrehearsed and spontaneous, the lay "amen" during the sermon is past all reviving, though it reflects a sure instinct in worship.

It would seem that at present spontaneity is not provided for in any way in most of Protestant worship. The concerns of the Church may provide a possibility for greater spontaneity. But it still remains to be seen if spontaneity is to regain much place in our worship.

It may sound premature to say that congregational singing is declining in Protestant churches though this seems to be true. It is even more ironical when we see many Roman Catholic congregations working to recover congregational singing. The singing in many Protestant churches is increasingly feeble and faltering. One notices many people standing in churches, a hymnal in their hands but with their mouths shut. How does one account for this failure to make a joyful sound or any sound at all?

Part of the problem, undoubtedly, is that of self-consciousness, and part that of laziness. People do not want to expose themselves, particularly their lack of musical ability. It only takes a few people, turning to look at someone singing enthusiastically, to make him cower and stop singing altogether. We forget too easily that though singing in tune is preferable, it is the act of offering one's praise in public that matters, and not the aesthetic quality of it. Too often we have left the singing to the choir, which has at least the semblance of talent. Congregational singing is not based upon talent but upon the response of praise of those singing. It provides an excellent means, perhaps the best single means, of expressing praise, and ought to be encouraged rather than allowed to go by default.

Congregational singing is not limited to hymns. There are some items that are ordinary parts of worship: responses, the *Gloria patri,* the *Gloria in excelsis,* the

Sanctus, and the *Agnus dei*. Too often these have been pre-empted altogether by the choir. Yet they belong to the congregation and there is no reason to deprive the congregation of these ordinary items.

There are several problems with regard to hymns. First there is the general indifference with regard to their teaching. Effective use can be made of the choir in teaching new hymns if one is really concerned. There is much to be said for an occasional hymn sing, or, as we say in our more sophisticated language, a festival of hymns. But there may be a deeper problem. Very few of the hymns we sing today were written in this century. Most of our hymnals rarely get past Gerard Manley Hopkins, if that far. Contemporary poetry refuses to abide by the restrictions of common meter and short meter. Poets today don't think in neat classical patterns. Most good poetry today tends to be free in its form and this is much more difficult to set to traditional music.

How can we bring good religious poetry and music together, or is it impossible? Is the hymn, as we now know it, an outdated art form? Quite possibly this is so, though we continue to produce traditional hymnals. Our present need might well be a quite different type of music that is free in form. Considerable success has been had in the congregational use of the Gelineau settings for the psalms.[7] Here a means has been found by which the free forms of the psalms are preserved in a singable way rather than by compressing them into metrical paraphrases. The way forward may be suggested by going back to singing the psalms. Such practice may point the way to a combination of contemporary religious poetry and music. We can

[7]Cf. *Thirty Psalms and Two Canticles* (Toledo: Gregorian Institute of America, 1956).

hardly expect the poet or the musician to return to the eighteenth century to present us with congregational singing for the twentieth century. In the meantime, we could do worse than to use the Gelineau settings of the psalms and go on experimenting from this point. Congregational singing is too important to sacrifice simply to preserve archaic musical forms.

Another area in which we are faced with harmful losses is in the actions and movements of worship. At a time when we ought to be realizing that worship is more than just words, we appear to be losing some of the most expressive actions of worship that we already have. Once again, it is often more a question of indifference and laziness than any deliberate decision.

We have often criticized revivalism for what it did to Christian worship. But there are some things we can learn from revivalism. It certainly was not theological sophistication that made revivalism so successful, but rather a practical psychology. Revivalism sometimes understood people better than it did theology. One of the lessons we can learn is revivalism's realization of the interaction of the body and the mind. This we seem too prone to forget.

We would probably not want to revive such forms as the altar call. But we might learn some lessons from it. The altar call gave people a concrete and direct way of expressing that God was acting in their worship and that they could take part in this action by offering themselves. It was a splendidly expressive way of committing themselves. We have not found a substitute for it. This is our loss. We cannot go back to the altar call and all the pleading associated with it. How can we devise a means for people sitting on foam rubber pews to express their offering of themselves without some physical expression of this committal?

In some denominations we even stand fair to lose the practice of going forward to the altar rail to receive communion. This is sometimes excused on the basis of saving time. If the service is well conducted and the building adequately designed, the time factor is negligible. Two ministers can give communion to several hundred people in a few minutes provided the ushers co-operate and time is not wasted on individual table dismissals. Table dismissals have done much harm in needlessly protracting the service. The substitution of pew communion is sometimes justified on the grounds that this makes it possible for all to commune at the same time and thus to show forth the unity of the congregation. But surely a matter of split-second timing is not of much importance when one realizes that communion is an act that unites us not just as a congregation but with Christians throughout both space and time. The idea of local unity is only a small part of the concept of communion fellowship.

The simple act of going forward to receive the body and blood of our Lord is one of the most expressive acts of Christian worship. One takes himself, just as he is, and goes forward to receive the elements of life transformed in Christ. It is most unfortunate that such an act should be lost from our worship, an act that often seems to transcend the capacity of words to express its meaning. The means of expressing our offering are so under-played in Protestant worship that this opportunity ought not be relinquished. Reception of communion around the altar-table also signifies fellowship. Fellowship and offering, as shown forth in the communicating at the altar-table, are more important than the single aspect of fellowship reflected in pew communion.

Evidently the English Independents (Congregationalists) were the first to adopt pew communion. Until well into the nineteenth century, Scottish Presbyterians moved to sit around tables set up in the aisles of the churches on communion Sunday, a practice still maintained in the Reformed churches in the Netherlands. The Presbyterians succumbed to pew communion in the nineteenth century, and now it seems that Methodists are beginning to do likewise. All ought to reconsider whether the comfort and convenience thus gained merits the sacrifice of one of the most significant actions on the part of the laity. The objections of the Independents to kneeling would be answered by the increasing practice of having the laity stand to receive the sacrament. Every effort should be made to keep or recover reception of communion gathered about the Lord's table rather than in the pews.

It may seem strange to some to include preaching under this topic of losses, but this very well may be the case. In recent years preaching has come under much heavy criticism. Ironically this has occurred at a moment when Roman Catholics are paying a great deal more attention to preaching. Yet the question deserves to be raised whether preaching is in danger, since it has been so severely criticized in recent years. Bishop J. A. T. Robinson lampoons it as speaking "six feet above contradiction,"[8] though he continues to do considerable preaching himself. Dean Joseph Mathews says, "that thing called preaching we do on Sunday morning, I think that is finished."[9]

Other challenges to preaching center around the biblical

[8] *The New Reformation?* (Philadelphia: Westminster Press, 1965), p. 52.
[9] *Together*, X (March, 1966), 50.

illiteracy of modern Christians, for whom preaching tends to be increasingly obscure and irrelevant.

Like all criticisms, these are not without merit. Preaching has suffered from a lack of congregational participation, both in expectation and response. Little has been done to encourage congregations to read and reflect upon the sermon text before the service. We do little to integrate education and worship. Adult classes might very well be designed around the lessons used in worship, at least where a lectionary (list of lessons fixed in advance) is used. A few experiments have been made in asking the congregation to contribute to the preaching of the Word after the sermon. A suitable invitation might be phrased: "And now you are invited to declare to this congregation further interpretation of God's Word as disclosed in this text." Such an act adds an element of spontaneity, but it must be made clear there should be no intention of refuting or praising the handling of the text in the sermon. The invitation is to expanded witness, not debate. There may be a need for discussion at a subsequent time, but not during worship.

Much of the criticism of preaching is not directed at preaching as such, but against bad examples of it. Preaching involves a risk, an extreme risk that the Word of God may be obscured by human vanity, sloth, and just plain clumsiness. But it still seems to be a risk worth taking. Much of the Old Testament is a record of God entrusting His Word to fallible men, and the New Testament is similar. One can justify some risks and this seems to be one of them.

"Preaching of the Word," the *Westminster Directory* says, "being the power of God unto Salvation, and one of the greatest and most excellent Works belonging to the

Ministry of the Gospell, should bee so performed, that the Workman need not bee ashamed, but may save himself, and those that heare him."[10] This old definition still rings true. Preaching makes the gospel contemporary. By showing us the past actions of God, it helps us to understand what He is doing today. No other form of communication has replaced the human voice and person in their ability to address men. Preaching contributes to the sacraments' power to communicate. Far from competing with others forms of communication, preaching is needed to bring them to their fullest power.

II

Not all loss is to be regretted nor are all gains to be greeted with joy. Some things that have come to be more and more typical of Protestant worship today are of questionable value. It is difficult to analyze many of these items since some are more a spirit, a *geist,* than the rubrics or text of a service. It is notoriously difficult to nail down the spirit of anything. Too often it is simply taken for granted. And anyone who tries to be specific runs the risk of finding his experiences don't quite match those of others. We shall try, however, to point out three characteristics of Protestant worship today that we could afford to lose: self-consciousness, professionalism, and aestheticism.

We have mentioned already the debilitating self-consciousness that seems to plague so much of Protestant worship. It has served to freeze worshipers so they act as if the only aspect of man's being to be displayed in worship is the intellect—and that in the negative fashion of

[10]Thompson (ed.), *Liturgies of the Western Church,* p. 363.

appearing critical of the sermon. Generally, it has left us largely passive worshipers. Self-consciousness keeps people from singing hymns audibly, from saying the prayers with any fervor, or from showing any too obvious involvement.

The result has been congregations that are increasingly inert, but that preserve their middle class self-consciousness at all odds. How this can be prevented is not easily answered. One suspects that no gimmicks or gadgets will succeed here and that the only hope of overcoming this self-consciousness is through a general renewal of the total life of the Church rather than just changing the forms of worship.

Part of the same problem is the increasing professionalism of Protestant worship, in which worship tends to be treated as the work of the experts whom the congregation listens to. Much of the decline of congregational singing has come about through turning parts of the service over to the choir. All too often the prayers are all taken by the clergy. Except for a few hymns, the creed, and the psalter, the whole service is performed by the ministers and the choir. Undoubtedly they do a smoother and more polished job.

But worship is an amateur job. At its best, worship is the work of the whole church and not just those with specialized training. Certainly some are set aside for particular functions in worship, but this by no means excludes the others. Any adequate doctrine of the Church must state that worship is the responsibility of the whole Church, not just the ministers. To speak of holy orders does not imply that the rest of the Church are in unholy orders. One man may have the responsibility to preach because his training and ordination prepare him to represent the whole Church to the congregation. But preaching remains the work of the whole congregation as the others seek to hear God's Word in, with, and under the words of the preacher. Worship is a do-it-yourself job not surrogated to others.

Recovering the amateur status of worship is essentially recovering a proper doctrine of the Church as consisting of the laity as much as the clergy. There is no place in the life of the Church where professionalism is quite so obvious as in worship. Worship is me doing it, but we tend, instead, to make worship the minister doing it. A more adequate manner of worship does not mean the minister and choir doing less, but the congregation as a whole more actively engaged in what the "professionals" now do. There is no act of worship in which the congregation should be passive. Even in the sermon each worshiper is listening to hear the Word of God for his life. Preaching is as active a part of the service as any.

We need to be less fastidious in our worship. Perhaps the congregation cannot sing as well as the choir. Is not it better that they make the effort instead of turning even the ordinary parts of the service over to the professionals? Unfortunately professionals resent the unpolished work of amateurs in every field of endeavor.

It might be well to compare the work of worship to that of the theater. In some of the best drama today the audience finds itself drawn into the action. The designs of new theaters diminish the distinction of acting space and audience space until sometimes they are inseparable. The audience finds that the action is about them and that they are on stage. This is what should happen in worship. The whole church building is a stage, and we are all actors with the professionals present to direct and to prompt us.

Worship is the work of the whole congregation and not just the professionals.

Closely allied to the problem of professionalism is that of aestheticism. Within Protestant churches, there seems at present to be a mighty crescendo of concern with aesthetics. Indeed it is quite the thing to do to boast of one's choir, to stage an art exhibit, and to have some unconventional drama staged, preferably in the chancel. We have become enraptured with the Christian year and the possibilities it opens for artistic expression. There is nothing wrong with all of this except that we have rarely thought through the role of art in worship, something we should have done first.

The role of the arts in worship is that of a handmaiden, or better still that of a servant. The Church is not the place to speak of "art for art's sake," an old war cry of some merit but totally irrelevant with regard to worship. The church is not a museum. Where art becomes an end in itself, it ought to be removed to another part of the building. When art calls attention to itself rather than providing the context for worship, it mistakes its function. The art used in worship, liturgical art as it is properly called, is very much needed. It is art that refers us to something beyond itself, to the object of our worship. Representations of Christ remind us of the divine activity in our worship and world. Genuine liturgical art is very much needed, since it prevents the idolatry of worship becoming a concentration only on ourselves and our needs.

But in our enthusiasm for art, have we stopped to raise the question whether we have understood its role in worship? Liturgical art is a highly specialized type of art. Religious art is not enough. Liturgics comes first, then aesthetics, when it comes to designing and adorning the place where worship is offered. There are good reasons for the use of liturgical art, but we ought to be concerned primarily about its functions in worship and this has often been neglected.

The problem of aesthetics becomes particularly acute with regard to church music. The use of the choir is one of the greatest problems with regard to the forms of Protestant worship today. We work energetically (and often successfully) to build bigger and better choirs without taking much time to consider the choir's function in worship. The choir is neither good nor bad, but the uses made of it can be good or bad. It is the failure to think through these uses that is the crux of the problem.

How often is the choir used as little more than entertainment for the congregation? Of course it is never put quite this bluntly, but the effect seems to be about this when the congregation settles back for a concert. The appreciation of beauty and worship are not necessarily identical activities. Equally bad is the use of the choir to provide atmosphere or to fill up awkward moments in the service.

Good and important functions of the choir include sharing in the proclamation of the Word, though this involves more care in the selection of text and music than is sometimes the case. Choral music understood as the offering to God of the talents of the choir has a great deal to commend it. And choirs could be used much more effectively in leading congregational singing, even if this means splitting up the group and infiltrating the congregation.

The chief question that must be raised in relation to the choir is: What can the choir do that the congregation cannot? In some cases the answer very well may be nothing. If so, one should have the courage to use a choir only for the occasional sacred concert. It is not enough to have a choir just because they sound nice or make the service more enjoyable. Music, like all the arts, appears in worship as a servant, and where it draws attention to itself must be banished from the premises.

One minor item needs to be mentioned, but in a way it symbolizes most of the preceding problems. This is the usual church pew. It is a comparative newcomer, having been introduced in the late Middle Ages. Until that time Christians stood for worship as they still do in some Eastern Orthodox churches. There is probably nothing wrong with sitting, at least for a part of worship. But one can raise some questions about the contemporary pew. Incidentally there is no reason to begrudge its comfort except as a negative symbol.[11] There is nothing particularly good about discomfort.

The problem of the pew is the rigid regimentation and the lack of flexibility that it entails. It is a curb on movement and suggests to the congregation a static role that they seem all too prone to adopt. There is no real reason for the congregation to be ranked in parallel rows stretching away from where the Word is preached and the sacrament celebrated. The people are not there as soldiers on dress parade but as men in action. Pews suggest too easily a static and passive approach to worship.

They make difficult, if not impossible, new configurations for worship. Perhaps the fewer things we have nailed down in our churches the better they would be. A service in which baptism is celebrated may demand a quite special configuration of the congregation, but this is impos-

[11]Pierre Berton, *The Comfortable Pew* (Philadelphia: Lippincott, 1965).

sible with pews. One has only one choice with pews and that often the worst possible. Then too, a church filled with pews is always part empty until the pews are full. Movable seating adapts the building for the number of worshipers. There is no need for chapels of varying size. Experiments in different types of liturgical arrangements are always possible and can change as our understanding of worship changes.

There are now available movable seats that are comfortable, attractive, easily stacked, easily linked, and reasonably priced. Use of movable seating can help the congregation gain a new impression of its role in worship and a new ability to adapt to changing forms of worship. Comfortable or otherwise, we could afford to lose the pew.

III

There are several areas of potential developments, of things Protestants are, or ought to be, gaining. The advent of some of these seems long overdue. One can sometimes see more of the future of Protestant worship by looking to the past. Second only to the study of theology of worship is the study of the history of worship. Much of the impetus for liturgical renewal in our time has been nourished by the study of the history of worship. Focus on the essentials in the eucharistic rite, the relations of baptism to confirmation, the role of the laity in worship, and many other areas have been illuminated by historical studies. Those things that have seemed valid in the past are not to be spurned. They have much to speak in judgment of us. At least we have a responsibility to the past that we have too long ignored. We are not called to romanticize the past. Every era had its drawbacks and there was no golden age of worship. We would not want to imitate the past, but at least the past can put to us questions we need to ask of our own time.

There are five areas especially needing Protestant attention in the future. These are areas of possible gain. Reflecting the experiences of the past, they seem to point out gains to be made in the future. The areas are: greater congregational participation, an understanding of worship as the action of both God and man, more emphasis on the sacraments, more theological discussion of worship, and a fuller understanding of the worldliness of worship.

We need not say much here about the need for more full-hearted congregation participation in worship. This is partly a matter of forms. Certainly some forms encourage this much more than others, as in the new liturgy of the Church of South India. Almost all recent liturgical revisions seem to point in this direction. But it will take more than rubrics and texts to bring this about. The congregation must come to see itself as a part of the whole Church in which all members join to offer their worship to God. It is not enough to print more parts of the service in bold type as the people's part. The people must be brought to understand and experience more fully their role as the worshiping Church, the Church within the Church. This is the Church that knows its Lord, that hears His voice.

All this implies a tremendous amount of teaching ministry. The New England Puritans were accustomed to appoint a teaching minister in many congregations with as much honor as the preaching minister. This would seem to be the role of the minister today, to spend a major portion of his time teaching what it is to be the Church. Only then will the congregation realize its active role in worship and fulfill it with understanding.

Closely allied to this is the need to think of worship as

an activity in which both God and man participate. Too often worship is approached from the dimension of man and what he may get out of it. Certainly man does stand to profit from worship but to approach it from this direction is to miss it altogether. Worship is offered to God for God's sake, and yet God works in worship for man's sake. We pray, yet "the Spirit intercedes" for us. God gives of Himself to us in worship and we offer ourselves to Him.

Worship is an activity in which God and man both work, God in giving Himself to man through the sacraments and through the Word. Man in return offers himself to God through prayer and the offering of his praise and gifts. Worship is a model of the world in which God gives His work to man and man performs his work as an offering to God. Both act in worship and both act in the world. God's creating activity continues and man serves his neighbor as his proper service to God. In worship man recognizes the true nature of his life and puts into representative words and actions what he does the rest of the week in other words and actions.

It is safe to predict that we will see more emphasis within Protestantism on the sacraments. There are sound theological and historical reasons for this renewed interest. There also seems to be sound psychological warrant for this too. No longer can we understand man as disembodied mind. What goes on in the body has major bearing on the mind. Worship that tried to be purely mental, dwelling exclusively in word symbols, simply neglected the nature of man. Too long we have trusted almost entirely to word symbols for communicating our worship.

We live in an era where television has made us more conscious than ever of the impact of the visual image.

Every indication is that communications will become more oriented to the visual image. Even our magazines have found it necessary to complement the verbal with the visual. Surely if the visual has been found so effective a means of communication in our time, worship should not ignore this communications revolution. The sacraments, with their visual imagery, are powerful means of communicating the gospel. In effect the Church knew all along what the communications researchers have now documented scientifically.

It should not be thought that the sacraments in any way undercut preaching. The sacraments demand preaching and preaching needs the sacraments. A greater emphasis on the sacraments means a corresponding emphasis on preaching. The minister preaches on some portion of the gospel each Sunday and then in the eucharist surveys the whole gospel. The sermon does what the sacrament cannot do, it contemporizes one particular aspect of the gospel. And the sacrament shows forth the heart of the gospel more tersely than any sermon could possibly do. Preaching and the sacraments are means whereby God accommodates Himself to us, giving Himself through both our intellect and our senses.

One of Protestantism's greatest needs with regard to worship is greatly expanded theological discussion. So far this area of the Church's activity has been overshadowed by the other interests of the major Protestant theologians of our time. Much of interest has appeared in the writings of such Roman Catholics as Casel, Schillebeeckx, Guardini, and Rahner. Protestantism needs much more theological attention to communicating in contemporary terms the meaning of worship.

But the task does not belong to the professional theologians alone. It is the duty of every Christian layman to raise questions about the meaning of worship. Often the raising of questions is more important than the answering of them. If this book can help prompt some of the questions it will have fulfilled its purpose. These are not questions easily put aside. If they were they would hardly be worth the effort. To seek an understanding of the meaning of our worship is the duty of any worshiper.

It has often been the case that this type of questioning and ensuing discussion can be a major factor in the renewal of the Church. Renewal, after all, is a gift from God. But we can provide its context. Theological discussion ought to be going on at all times with regard to all aspects of life. Worship is a central activity of the Church, and in many instances of Church renewal it has become even more so. There is a pressing need for more searching and probing with regard to the meaning of worship in order for the Church to understand itself. Discussion in depth of the meaning of worship can be one of the best means of the Church's rediscovery of its mission in the world today.

Finally, it is greatly to be hoped that the worldliness of worship will be more apparent to Christians. Many writers about the Church and the modern world have little or nothing to say about worship. Worship often seems to them an idle pastime or worse, a fiddling while the world burns. No doubt the attitude of most Christians has been to regard worship as divorced from any sense of responsibility to the world. Too often Christian worship has been the "noise of solemn assemblies," unconcerned with the world outside. Those tending to discount worship can hardly be blamed. Most worshipers apparently feel the same way about the irrelevancy of worship as those who break into print about it.

In actuality, worship has a great deal to do with the world. Worship is worldly to the core. The great importance of worship is that it encounters the world in a dimension of depth not likely to be duplicated in any other activity. Christian worship takes the world seriously because the God it encounters is a worldly God. Worship sends men into service in the world where they act in the sphere of God's activity.

Far from taking men out of the world, worship makes them understand that the only possibility of serving God is by fulfilling our servanthood in the world where God is at work in the midst of His creation. Worship makes us more worldly by helping us encounter the world at a deeper level.